The Knight's Tale

By Geoffrey Chaucer

Translated by David Laing Purves, Born 1838 – Died 1873

Includes MLA Style Citations for Scholarly Secondary Sources, Peer-Reviewed Journal Articles and Critical Essays

The Knight's Tale

By Geoffrey Chaucer

Translated by David Laing Purves, Born 1838 – Died 1873

A Squid Ink Classic

[Squid Ink Classics Edition]

January 2017

Boston, MA

THE KNIGHT'S TALE <1>

WHILOM*, as olde stories tellen us, *formerly
There was a duke that highte* Theseus. *was called <2>
Of Athens he was lord and governor,
And in his time such a conqueror
That greater was there none under the sun.
Full many a riche country had he won.
What with his wisdom and his chivalry,
He conquer'd all the regne of Feminie,<3>
That whilom was y-cleped Scythia;
And weddede the Queen Hippolyta
And brought her home with him to his country
With muchel* glory and great solemnity, *great
And eke her younge sister Emily,
And thus with vict'ry and with melody
Let I this worthy Duke to Athens ride,
And all his host, in armes him beside.

And certes, if it n'ere* too long to hear, *were not
I would have told you fully the mannere,
How wonnen* was the regne of Feminie, <4> *won
By Theseus, and by his chivalry;
And of the greate battle for the nonce
Betwixt Athenes and the Amazons;
And how assieged was Hippolyta,
The faire hardy queen of Scythia;
And of the feast that was at her wedding
And of the tempest at her homecoming.
But all these things I must as now forbear.
I have, God wot, a large field to ear* *plough<5>;
And weake be the oxen in my plough;
The remnant of my tale is long enow.
I will not *letten eke none of this rout*. *hinder any of

Let every fellow tell his tale about, this company*
And let see now who shall the supper win.
There *as I left*, I will again begin. *where I left off*

This Duke, of whom I make mentioun,
When he was come almost unto the town,
In all his weal, and in his moste pride,
He was ware, as he cast his eye aside,
Where that there kneeled in the highe way
A company of ladies, tway and tway,
Each after other, clad in clothes black:
But such a cry and such a woe they make,
That in this world n'is creature living,
That hearde such another waimenting* *lamenting <6>
And of this crying would they never stenten*, *desist
Till they the reines of his bridle henten*. *seize
"What folk be ye that at mine homecoming
Perturben so my feaste with crying?"
Quoth Theseus; "Have ye so great envy
Of mine honour, that thus complain and cry?
Or who hath you misboden*, or offended? *wronged
Do telle me, if it may be amended;
And why that ye be clad thus all in black?"

The oldest lady of them all then spake,
When she had swooned, with a deadly cheer*, *countenance
That it was ruthe* for to see or hear. *pity
She saide; "Lord, to whom fortune hath given
Vict'ry, and as a conqueror to liven,
Nought grieveth us your glory and your honour;
But we beseechen mercy and succour.
Have mercy on our woe and our distress;
Some drop of pity, through thy gentleness,
Upon us wretched women let now fall.

For certes, lord, there is none of us all
That hath not been a duchess or a queen;
Now be we caitives*, as it is well seen: *captives
Thanked be Fortune, and her false wheel,
That *none estate ensureth to be wele*. *assures no
continuance of
And certes, lord, t'abiden your presence prosperous estate*
Here in this temple of the goddess Clemence
We have been waiting all this fortenight:
Now help us, lord, since it lies in thy might.

"I, wretched wight, that weep and waile thus,
Was whilom wife to king Capaneus,
That starf* at Thebes, cursed be that day: *died <7>
And alle we that be in this array,
And maken all this lamentatioun,
We losten all our husbands at that town,
While that the siege thereabouten lay.
And yet the olde Creon, wellaway!
That lord is now of Thebes the city,
Fulfilled of ire and of iniquity,
He for despite, and for his tyranny,
To do the deade bodies villainy*, *insult
Of all our lorde's, which that been y-slaw, *slain
Hath all the bodies on an heap y-draw,
And will not suffer them by none assent
Neither to be y-buried, nor y-brent*, *burnt
But maketh houndes eat them in despite."
And with that word, withoute more respite
They fallen groff,* and cryden piteously; *grovelling
"Have on us wretched women some mercy,
And let our sorrow sinken in thine heart."

This gentle Duke down from his courser start
With hearte piteous, when he heard them speak.
Him thoughte that his heart would all to-break,
When he saw them so piteous and so mate* *abased
That whilom weren of so great estate.
And in his armes he them all up hent*, *raised, took
And them comforted in full good intent,
And swore his oath, as he was true knight,
He woulde do *so farforthly his might* *as far as his power
went*
Upon the tyrant Creon them to wreak*, *avenge
That all the people of Greece shoulde speak,
How Creon was of Theseus y-served,
As he that had his death full well deserved.
And right anon withoute more abode* *delay
His banner he display'd, and forth he rode
To Thebes-ward, and all his, host beside:
No ner* Athenes would he go nor ride, *nearer
Nor take his ease fully half a day,
But onward on his way that night he lay:
And sent anon Hippolyta the queen,
And Emily her younge sister sheen* *bright, lovely
Unto the town of Athens for to dwell:
And forth he rit*; there is no more to tell. *rode

The red statue of Mars with spear and targe* *shield
So shineth in his white banner large
That all the fieldes glitter up and down:
And by his banner borne is his pennon
Of gold full rich, in which there was y-beat* *stamped
The Minotaur<8> which that he slew in Crete
Thus rit this Duke, thus rit this conqueror
And in his host of chivalry the flower,
Till that he came to Thebes, and alight

Fair in a field, there as he thought to fight.
But shortly for to speaken of this thing,
With Creon, which that was of Thebes king,
He fought, and slew him manly as a knight
In plain bataille, and put his folk to flight:
And by assault he won the city after,
And rent adown both wall, and spar, and rafter;
And to the ladies he restored again
The bodies of their husbands that were slain,
To do obsequies, as was then the guise*. *custom

But it were all too long for to devise* *describe
The greate clamour, and the waimenting*, *lamenting
Which that the ladies made at the brenning* *burning
Of the bodies, and the great honour
That Theseus the noble conqueror
Did to the ladies, when they from him went:
But shortly for to tell is mine intent.
When that this worthy Duke, this Theseus,
Had Creon slain, and wonnen Thebes thus,
Still in the field he took all night his rest,
And did with all the country as him lest*. *pleased
To ransack in the tas* of bodies dead, *heap
Them for to strip of *harness and of **weed, *armour
**clothes
The pillers* did their business and cure, *pillagers <9>
After the battle and discomfiture.
And so befell, that in the tas they found,
Through girt with many a grievous bloody wound,
Two younge knightes *ligging by and by* *lying side by
side*
Both in *one armes*, wrought full richely: *the same
armour*
Of whiche two, Arcita hight that one,

And he that other highte Palamon.
Not fully quick*, nor fully dead they were, *alive
But by their coat-armour, and by their gear,
The heralds knew them well in special,
As those that weren of the blood royal
Of Thebes, and *of sistren two y-born*. *born of two
sisters*
Out of the tas the pillers have them torn,
And have them carried soft unto the tent
Of Theseus, and he full soon them sent
To Athens, for to dwellen in prison
Perpetually, he *n'olde no ranson*. *would take no ransom*
And when this worthy Duke had thus y-done,
He took his host, and home he rit anon
With laurel crowned as a conquerour;
And there he lived in joy and in honour
Term of his life; what needeth wordes mo'?
And in a tower, in anguish and in woe,
Dwellen this Palamon, and eke Arcite,
For evermore, there may no gold them quite* *set free

Thus passed year by year, and day by day,
Till it fell ones in a morn of May
That Emily, that fairer was to seen
Than is the lily upon his stalke green,
And fresher than the May with flowers new
(For with the rose colour strove her hue;
I n'ot* which was the finer of them two), *know not
Ere it was day, as she was wont to do,
She was arisen, and all ready dight*, *dressed
For May will have no sluggardy a-night;
The season pricketh every gentle heart,
And maketh him out of his sleep to start,
And saith, "Arise, and do thine observance."

This maketh Emily have remembrance
To do honour to May, and for to rise.
Y-clothed was she fresh for to devise;
Her yellow hair was braided in a tress,
Behind her back, a yarde long I guess.
And in the garden at *the sun uprist* *sunrise
She walketh up and down where as her list.
She gathereth flowers, party* white and red, *mingled
To make a sotel* garland for her head, *subtle, well-arranged
And as an angel heavenly she sung.
The greate tower, that was so thick and strong,
Which of the castle was the chief dungeon<10>
(Where as these knightes weren in prison,
Of which I tolde you, and telle shall),
Was even joinant* to the garden wall, *adjoining
There as this Emily had her playing.

Bright was the sun, and clear that morrowning,
And Palamon, this woful prisoner,
As was his wont, by leave of his gaoler,
Was ris'n, and roamed in a chamber on high,
In which he all the noble city sigh*, *saw
And eke the garden, full of branches green,
There as this fresh Emelia the sheen
Was in her walk, and roamed up and down.
This sorrowful prisoner, this Palamon
Went in his chamber roaming to and fro,
And to himself complaining of his woe:
That he was born, full oft he said, Alas!
And so befell, by aventure or cas*, *chance
That through a window thick of many a bar
Of iron great, and square as any spar,
He cast his eyes upon Emelia,
And therewithal he blent* and cried, Ah! *started aside

As though he stungen were unto the heart.
And with that cry Arcite anon up start,
And saide, "Cousin mine, what aileth thee,
That art so pale and deadly for to see?
Why cried'st thou? who hath thee done offence?
For Godde's love, take all in patience
Our prison*, for it may none other be. *imprisonment
Fortune hath giv'n us this adversity'.
Some wick'* aspect or disposition *wicked
Of Saturn<11>, by some constellation,
Hath giv'n us this, although we had it sworn,
So stood the heaven when that we were born,
We must endure; this is the short and plain.

This Palamon answer'd, and said again:
"Cousin, forsooth of this opinion
Thou hast a vain imagination.
This prison caused me not for to cry;
But I was hurt right now thorough mine eye
Into mine heart; that will my bane* be. *destruction
The fairness of the lady that I see
Yond in the garden roaming to and fro,
Is cause of all my crying and my woe.
I *n'ot wher* she be woman or goddess, *know not whether*
But Venus is it, soothly* as I guess, *truly
And therewithal on knees adown he fill,
And saide: "Venus, if it be your will
You in this garden thus to transfigure
Before me sorrowful wretched creature,
Out of this prison help that we may scape.
And if so be our destiny be shape
By etern word to dien in prison,
Of our lineage have some compassion,
That is so low y-brought by tyranny."

And with that word Arcita *gan espy* *began to look forth*
Where as this lady roamed to and fro
And with that sight her beauty hurt him so,
That if that Palamon was wounded sore,
Arcite is hurt as much as he, or more.
And with a sigh he saide piteously:
"The freshe beauty slay'th me suddenly
Of her that roameth yonder in the place.
And but* I have her mercy and her grace, *unless
That I may see her at the leaste way,
I am but dead; there is no more to say."
This Palamon, when he these wordes heard,
Dispiteously* he looked, and answer'd: *angrily
"Whether say'st thou this in earnest or in play?"
"Nay," quoth Arcite, "in earnest, by my fay*. *faith
God help me so, *me lust full ill to play*." *I am in no
humour
This Palamon gan knit his browes tway. for jesting*
"It were," quoth he, "to thee no great honour
For to be false, nor for to be traitour
To me, that am thy cousin and thy brother
Y-sworn full deep, and each of us to other,
That never for to dien in the pain <12>,
Till that the death departen shall us twain,
Neither of us in love to hinder other,
Nor in none other case, my leve* brother; *dear
But that thou shouldest truly farther me
In every case, as I should farther thee.
This was thine oath, and mine also certain;
I wot it well, thou dar'st it not withsayn*, *deny
Thus art thou of my counsel out of doubt,
And now thou wouldest falsely be about
To love my lady, whom I love and serve,
And ever shall, until mine hearte sterve* *die

13

Now certes, false Arcite, thou shalt not so
I lov'd her first, and tolde thee my woe
As to my counsel, and my brother sworn
To farther me, as I have told beforn.
For which thou art y-bounden as a knight
To helpe me, if it lie in thy might,
Or elles art thou false, I dare well sayn,"

This Arcita full proudly spake again:
"Thou shalt," quoth he, "be rather* false than I, *sooner
And thou art false, I tell thee utterly;
For par amour I lov'd her first ere thou.
What wilt thou say? *thou wist it not right now* *even now thou
Whether she be a woman or goddess. knowest not*
Thine is affection of holiness,
And mine is love, as to a creature:
For which I tolde thee mine aventure
As to my cousin, and my brother sworn
I pose*, that thou loved'st her beforn: *suppose
Wost* thou not well the olde clerke's saw<13>, *know'st
That who shall give a lover any law?
Love is a greater lawe, by my pan,
Than may be giv'n to any earthly man:
Therefore positive law, and such decree,
Is broke alway for love in each degree
A man must needes love, maugre his head.
He may not flee it, though he should be dead,
All be she maid, or widow, or else wife. *whether she be*
And eke it is not likely all thy life
To standen in her grace, no more than I
For well thou wost thyselfe verily,
That thou and I be damned to prison
Perpetual, us gaineth no ranson.

We strive, as did the houndes for the bone;
They fought all day, and yet their part was none.
There came a kite, while that they were so wroth,
And bare away the bone betwixt them both.
And therefore at the kinge's court, my brother,
Each man for himselfe, there is no other.
Love if thee list; for I love and aye shall
And soothly, leve brother, this is all.
Here in this prison musten we endure,
And each of us take his Aventure."

Great was the strife and long between these tway,
If that I hadde leisure for to say;
But to the effect: it happen'd on a day
(To tell it you as shortly as I may),
A worthy duke that hight Perithous<14>
That fellow was to the Duke Theseus
Since thilke* day that they were children lite**   *that **little
Was come to Athens, his fellow to visite,
And for to play, as he was wont to do;
For in this world he loved no man so;
And he lov'd him as tenderly again.
So well they lov'd, as olde bookes sayn,
That when that one was dead, soothly to sayn,
His fellow went and sought him down in hell:
But of that story list me not to write.
Duke Perithous loved well Arcite,
And had him known at Thebes year by year:
And finally at request and prayere
Of Perithous, withoute ranson
Duke Theseus him let out of prison,
Freely to go, where him list over all,
In such a guise, as I you tellen shall
This was the forword*, plainly to indite,   *promise

Betwixte Theseus and him Arcite:
That if so were, that Arcite were y-found
Ever in his life, by day or night, one stound* *moment<15>
In any country of this Theseus,
And he were caught, it was accorded thus,
That with a sword he shoulde lose his head;
There was none other remedy nor rede*. *counsel
But took his leave, and homeward he him sped;
Let him beware, his necke lieth *to wed*. *in pledge*

How great a sorrow suff'reth now Arcite!
The death he feeleth through his hearte smite;
He weepeth, waileth, crieth piteously;
To slay himself he waiteth privily.
He said; "Alas the day that I was born!
Now is my prison worse than beforn:
Now is me shape eternally to dwell *it is fixed for me*
Not in purgatory, but right in hell.
Alas! that ever I knew Perithous.
For elles had I dwelt with Theseus
Y-fettered in his prison evermo'.
Then had I been in bliss, and not in woe.
Only the sight of her, whom that I serve,
Though that I never may her grace deserve,
Would have sufficed right enough for me.
O deare cousin Palamon," quoth he,
"Thine is the vict'ry of this aventure,
Full blissfully in prison to endure:
In prison? nay certes, in paradise.
Well hath fortune y-turned thee the dice,
That hast the sight of her, and I th' absence.
For possible is, since thou hast her presence,
And art a knight, a worthy and an able,
That by some cas*, since fortune is changeable, *chance

16

Thou may'st to thy desire sometime attain.
But I that am exiled, and barren
Of alle grace, and in so great despair,
That there n'is earthe, water, fire, nor air,
Nor creature, that of them maked is,
That may me helpe nor comfort in this,
Well ought I *sterve in wanhope* and distress. *die in despair*
Farewell my life, my lust*, and my gladness. *pleasure
Alas, *why plainen men so in commune *why do men so often complain
Of purveyance of God*, or of Fortune, of God's providence?*
That giveth them full oft in many a guise
Well better than they can themselves devise?
Some man desireth for to have richess,
That cause is of his murder or great sickness.
And some man would out of his prison fain,
That in his house is of his meinie* slain. *servants <16>
Infinite harmes be in this mattere.
We wot never what thing we pray for here.
We fare as he that drunk is as a mouse.
A drunken man wot well he hath an house,
But he wot not which is the right way thither,
And to a drunken man the way is slither*. *slippery
And certes in this world so fare we.
We seeke fast after felicity,
But we go wrong full often truely.
Thus we may sayen all, and namely* I, *especially
That ween'd*, and had a great opinion, *thought
That if I might escape from prison
Then had I been in joy and perfect heal,
Where now I am exiled from my weal.

Since that I may not see you, Emily,
I am but dead; there is no remedy."

Upon that other side, Palamon,
When that he wist Arcita was agone,
Much sorrow maketh, that the greate tower
Resounded of his yelling and clamour
The pure* fetters on his shinnes great   *very <17>
Were of his bitter salte teares wet.

"Alas!" quoth he, "Arcita, cousin mine,
Of all our strife, God wot, the fruit is thine.
Thou walkest now in Thebes at thy large,
And of my woe thou *givest little charge*. *takest little
heed*
Thou mayst, since thou hast wisdom and manhead*,
*manhood, courage
Assemble all the folk of our kindred,
And make a war so sharp on this country
That by some aventure, or some treaty,
Thou mayst have her to lady and to wife,
For whom that I must needes lose my life.
For as by way of possibility,
Since thou art at thy large, of prison free,
And art a lord, great is thine avantage,
More than is mine, that sterve here in a cage.
For I must weep and wail, while that I live,
With all the woe that prison may me give,
And eke with pain that love me gives also,
That doubles all my torment and my woe."

Therewith the fire of jealousy upstart
Within his breast, and hent* him by the heart *seized
So woodly*, that he like was to behold *madly
The box-tree, or the ashes dead and cold.

18

Then said; "O cruel goddess, that govern
This world with binding of your word etern* *eternal
And writen in the table of adamant
Your parlement* and your eternal grant, *consultation
What is mankind more *unto you y-hold* *by you esteemed
Than is the sheep, that rouketh* in the fold! *lie huddled
together
For slain is man, right as another beast;
And dwelleth eke in prison and arrest,
And hath sickness, and great adversity,
And oftentimes guilteless, pardie* *by God
What governance is in your prescience,
That guilteless tormenteth innocence?
And yet increaseth this all my penance,
That man is bounden to his observance
For Godde's sake to *letten of his will*, *restrain his desire*
Whereas a beast may all his lust fulfil.
And when a beast is dead, he hath no pain;
But man after his death must weep and plain,
Though in this worlde he have care and woe:
Withoute doubt it maye standen so.
"The answer of this leave I to divines,
But well I wot, that in this world great pine* is; *pain,
trouble
Alas! I see a serpent or a thief
That many a true man hath done mischief,
Go at his large, and where him list may turn.
But I must be in prison through Saturn,
And eke through Juno, jealous and eke wood*, *mad
That hath well nigh destroyed all the blood
Of Thebes, with his waste walles wide.
And Venus slay'th me on that other side
For jealousy, and fear of him, Arcite."

Now will I stent* of Palamon a lite**,   *pause **little
And let him in his prison stille dwell,
And of Arcita forth I will you tell.
The summer passeth, and the nightes long
Increase double-wise the paines strong
Both of the lover and the prisonere.
I n'ot* which hath the wofuller mistere**.   *know not
**condition
For, shortly for to say, this Palamon
Perpetually is damned to prison,
In chaines and in fetters to be dead;
And Arcite is exiled *on his head*   *on peril of his head*
For evermore as out of that country,
Nor never more he shall his lady see.
You lovers ask I now this question,<18>
Who lieth the worse, Arcite or Palamon?
The one may see his lady day by day,
But in prison he dwelle must alway.
The other where him list may ride or go,
But see his lady shall he never mo'.
Now deem all as you liste, ye that can,
For I will tell you forth as I began.

When that Arcite to Thebes comen was,
Full oft a day he swelt*, and said, "Alas!"   *fainted
For see this lady he shall never mo'.
And shortly to concluden all his woe,
So much sorrow had never creature
That is or shall be while the world may dure.
His sleep, his meat, his drink is *him byraft*,   *taken away
from him*
That lean he wex*, and dry as any shaft.   *became
His eyen hollow, grisly to behold,
His hue sallow, and pale as ashes cold,

20

And solitary he was, ever alone,
And wailing all the night, making his moan.
And if he hearde song or instrument,
Then would he weepen, he might not be stent*. *stopped
So feeble were his spirits, and so low,
And changed so, that no man coulde know
His speech, neither his voice, though men it heard.
And in his gear* for all the world he far'd *behaviour <19>
Not only like the lovers' malady
Of Eros, but rather y-like manie* *madness
Engender'd of humours melancholic,
Before his head in his cell fantastic.<20>
And shortly turned was all upside down,
Both habit and eke dispositioun,
Of him, this woful lover Dan* Arcite. *Lord <21>
Why should I all day of his woe indite?
When he endured had a year or two
This cruel torment, and this pain and woe,
At Thebes, in his country, as I said,
Upon a night in sleep as he him laid,
Him thought how that the winged god Mercury
Before him stood, and bade him to be merry.
His sleepy yard* in hand he bare upright; *rod <22>
A hat he wore upon his haires bright.
Arrayed was this god (as he took keep*) *notice
As he was when that Argus<23> took his sleep;
And said him thus: "To Athens shalt thou wend*; *go
There is thee shapen* of thy woe an end." *fixed, prepared
And with that word Arcite woke and start.
"Now truely how sore that e'er me smart,"
Quoth he, "to Athens right now will I fare.
Nor for no dread of death shall I not spare
To see my lady that I love and serve;
In her presence *I recke not to sterve.*" *do not care if I die*

And with that word he caught a great mirror,
And saw that changed was all his colour,
And saw his visage all in other kind.
And right anon it ran him ill his mind,
That since his face was so disfigur'd
Of malady the which he had endur'd,
He mighte well, if that he *bare him low,* *lived in lowly
fashion*
Live in Athenes evermore unknow,
And see his lady wellnigh day by day.
And right anon he changed his array,
And clad him as a poore labourer.
And all alone, save only a squier,
That knew his privity* and all his cas**, *secrets **fortune
Which was disguised poorly as he was,
To Athens is he gone the nexte* way. *nearest <24>
And to the court he went upon a day,
And at the gate he proffer'd his service,
To drudge and draw, what so men would devise*. *order
And, shortly of this matter for to sayn,
He fell in office with a chamberlain,
The which that dwelling was with Emily.
For he was wise, and coulde soon espy
Of every servant which that served her.
Well could he hewe wood, and water bear,
For he was young and mighty for the nones*, *occasion
And thereto he was strong and big of bones
To do that any wight can him devise.

A year or two he was in this service,
Page of the chamber of Emily the bright;
And Philostrate he saide that he hight.
But half so well belov'd a man as he
Ne was there never in court of his degree.

He was so gentle of conditioun,
That throughout all the court was his renown.
They saide that it were a charity
That Theseus would *enhance his degree*, *elevate him in
rank*
And put him in some worshipful service,
There as he might his virtue exercise.
And thus within a while his name sprung
Both of his deedes, and of his good tongue,
That Theseus hath taken him so near,
That of his chamber he hath made him squire,
And gave him gold to maintain his degree;
And eke men brought him out of his country
From year to year full privily his rent.
But honestly and slyly* he it spent, *discreetly, prudently
That no man wonder'd how that he it had.
And three year in this wise his life be lad*, *led
And bare him so in peace and eke in werre*, *war
There was no man that Theseus had so derre*. *dear
And in this blisse leave I now Arcite,
And speak I will of Palamon a lite*. *little

In darkness horrible, and strong prison,
This seven year hath sitten Palamon,
Forpined*, what for love, and for distress. *pined, wasted
away
Who feeleth double sorrow and heaviness
But Palamon? that love distraineth* so, *afflicts
That wood* out of his wits he went for woe, *mad
And eke thereto he is a prisonere
Perpetual, not only for a year.
Who coulde rhyme in English properly
His martyrdom? forsooth*, it is not I; *truly
Therefore I pass as lightly as I may.

23

It fell that in the seventh year, in May
The thirde night (as olde bookes sayn,
That all this story tellen more plain),
Were it by a venture or destiny
(As when a thing is shapen* it shall be), *settled, decreed
That soon after the midnight, Palamon
By helping of a friend brake his prison,
And fled the city fast as he might go,
For he had given drink his gaoler so
Of a clary <25>, made of a certain wine,
With *narcotise and opie* of Thebes fine, *narcotics and
opium*
That all the night, though that men would him shake,
The gaoler slept, he mighte not awake:
And thus he fled as fast as ever he may.
The night was short, and *faste by the day *close at hand
was
That needes cast he must himself to hide*. the day during
which
And to a grove faste there beside he must cast about, or
contrive,
With dreadful foot then stalked Palamon. to conceal
himself.*
For shortly this was his opinion,
That in the grove he would him hide all day,
And in the night then would he take his way
To Thebes-ward, his friendes for to pray
On Theseus to help him to warray*. *make war <26>
And shortly either he would lose his life,
Or winnen Emily unto his wife.
This is th' effect, and his intention plain.

Now will I turn to Arcita again,
That little wist how nighe was his care,

Till that Fortune had brought him in the snare.
The busy lark, the messenger of day,
Saluteth in her song the morning gray;
And fiery Phoebus riseth up so bright,
That all the orient laugheth at the sight,
And with his streames* drieth in the greves** *rays
**groves
The silver droppes, hanging on the leaves;
And Arcite, that is in the court royal
With Theseus, his squier principal,
Is ris'n, and looketh on the merry day.
And for to do his observance to May,
Remembering the point* of his desire, *object
He on his courser, starting as the fire,
Is ridden to the fieldes him to play,
Out of the court, were it a mile or tway.
And to the grove, of which I have you told,
By a venture his way began to hold,
To make him a garland of the greves*, *groves
Were it of woodbine, or of hawthorn leaves,
And loud he sang against the sun so sheen*. *shining bright
"O May, with all thy flowers and thy green,
Right welcome be thou, faire freshe May,
I hope that I some green here getten may."
And from his courser*, with a lusty heart, *horse
Into the grove full hastily he start,
And in a path he roamed up and down,
There as by aventure this Palamon
Was in a bush, that no man might him see,
For sore afeard of his death was he.
Nothing ne knew he that it was Arcite;
God wot he would have *trowed it full lite*. *full little
believed it*
But sooth is said, gone since full many years,

The field hath eyen*, and the wood hath ears, *eyes
It is full fair a man *to bear him even*, *to be on his guard*
For all day meeten men at *unset steven*. *unexpected time
<27>
Full little wot Arcite of his fellaw,
That was so nigh to hearken of his saw*, *saying, speech
For in the bush he sitteth now full still.
When that Arcite had roamed all his fill,
And *sungen all the roundel* lustily, *sang the
roundelay*<28>
Into a study he fell suddenly,
As do those lovers in their *quainte gears*, *odd fashions*
Now in the crop*, and now down in the breres**, <29>
*tree-top
Now up, now down, as bucket in a well. **briars
Right as the Friday, soothly for to tell,
Now shineth it, and now it raineth fast,
Right so can geary* Venus overcast *changeful
The heartes of her folk, right as her day
Is gearful*, right so changeth she array. *changeful
Seldom is Friday all the weeke like.
When Arcite had y-sung, he gan to sike*, *sigh
And sat him down withouten any more:
"Alas!" quoth he, "the day that I was bore!
How longe, Juno, through thy cruelty
Wilt thou warrayen* Thebes the city? *torment
Alas! y-brought is to confusion
The blood royal of Cadm' and Amphion:
Of Cadmus, which that was the firste man,
That Thebes built, or first the town began,
And of the city first was crowned king.
Of his lineage am I, and his offspring
By very line, as of the stock royal;
And now I am *so caitiff and so thrall*, *wretched and

26

enslaved*
That he that is my mortal enemy,
I serve him as his squier poorely.
And yet doth Juno me well more shame,
For I dare not beknow* mine owen name, *acknowledge
<30>
But there as I was wont to hight Arcite,
Now hight I Philostrate, not worth a mite.
Alas! thou fell Mars, and alas! Juno,
Thus hath your ire our lineage all fordo* *undone, ruined
Save only me, and wretched Palamon,
That Theseus martyreth in prison.
And over all this, to slay me utterly,
Love hath his fiery dart so brenningly* *burningly
Y-sticked through my true careful heart,
That shapen was my death erst than my shert. <31>
Ye slay me with your eyen, Emily;
Ye be the cause wherefore that I die.
Of all the remnant of mine other care
Ne set I not the *mountance of a tare*, *value of a straw*
So that I could do aught to your pleasance."

And with that word he fell down in a trance
A longe time; and afterward upstart
This Palamon, that thought thorough his heart
He felt a cold sword suddenly to glide:
For ire he quoke*, no longer would he hide. *quaked
And when that he had heard Arcite's tale,
As he were wood*, with face dead and pale, *mad
He start him up out of the bushes thick,
And said: "False Arcita, false traitor wick'*, *wicked
Now art thou hent*, that lov'st my lady so, *caught
For whom that I have all this pain and woe,
And art my blood, and to my counsel sworn,

As I full oft have told thee herebeforn,
And hast bejaped* here Duke Theseus, *deceived, imposed
upon
And falsely changed hast thy name thus;
I will be dead, or elles thou shalt die.
Thou shalt not love my lady Emily,
But I will love her only and no mo';
For I am Palamon thy mortal foe.
And though I have no weapon in this place,
But out of prison am astart* by grace, *escaped
I dreade* not that either thou shalt die, *doubt
Or else thou shalt not loven Emily.
Choose which thou wilt, for thou shalt not astart."

This Arcite then, with full dispiteous* heart, *wrathful
When he him knew, and had his tale heard,
As fierce as lion pulled out a swerd,
And saide thus; "By God that sitt'th above,
N'ere it that thou art sick, and wood for love, *were it not*
And eke that thou no weap'n hast in this place,
Thou should'st never out of this grove pace,
That thou ne shouldest dien of mine hand.
For I defy the surety and the band,
Which that thou sayest I have made to thee.
What? very fool, think well that love is free;
And I will love her maugre* all thy might. *despite
But, for thou art a worthy gentle knight,
And *wilnest to darraine her by bataille*, *will reclaim her
Have here my troth, to-morrow I will not fail, by combat*
Without weeting* of any other wight, *knowledge
That here I will be founden as a knight,
And bringe harness* right enough for thee; *armour and
arms
And choose the best, and leave the worst for me.

28

And meat and drinke this night will I bring
Enough for thee, and clothes for thy bedding.
And if so be that thou my lady win,
And slay me in this wood that I am in,
Thou may'st well have thy lady as for me."
This Palamon answer'd, "I grant it thee."
And thus they be departed till the morrow,
When each of them hath *laid his faith to borrow*. *pledged
his faith*

O Cupid, out of alle charity!
O Regne* that wilt no fellow have with thee! *queen <32>
Full sooth is said, that love nor lordeship
Will not, *his thanks*, have any fellowship. *thanks to him*
Well finden that Arcite and Palamon.
Arcite is ridd anon unto the town,
And on the morrow, ere it were daylight,
Full privily two harness hath he dight*, *prepared
Both suffisant and meete to darraine* *contest
The battle in the field betwixt them twain.
And on his horse, alone as he was born,
He carrieth all this harness him beforn;
And in the grove, at time and place y-set,
This Arcite and this Palamon be met.
Then change gan the colour of their face;
Right as the hunter in the regne* of Thrace *kingdom
That standeth at a gappe with a spear
When hunted is the lion or the bear,
And heareth him come rushing in the greves*, *groves
And breaking both the boughes and the leaves,
Thinketh, "Here comes my mortal enemy,
Withoute fail, he must be dead or I;
For either I must slay him at the gap;
Or he must slay me, if that me mishap:"

So fared they, in changing of their hue
As far as either of them other knew. *When they recognised each
There was no good day, and no saluting, other afar off*
But straight, withoute wordes rehearsing,
Evereach of them holp to arm the other,
As friendly, as he were his owen brother.
And after that, with sharpe speares strong
They foined* each at other wonder long. *thrust
Thou mightest weene*, that this Palamon *think
In fighting were as a wood* lion, *mad
And as a cruel tiger was Arcite:
As wilde boars gan they together smite,
That froth as white as foam, *for ire wood*. *mad with anger*
Up to the ancle fought they in their blood.
And in this wise I let them fighting dwell,
And forth I will of Theseus you tell.

The Destiny, minister general,
That executeth in the world o'er all
The purveyance*, that God hath seen beforn; *foreordination
So strong it is, that though the world had sworn
The contrary of a thing by yea or nay,
Yet some time it shall fallen on a day
That falleth not eft* in a thousand year. *again
For certainly our appetites here,
Be it of war, or peace, or hate, or love,
All is this ruled by the sight* above. *eye, intelligence, power
This mean I now by mighty Theseus,
That for to hunten is so desirous —
And namely* the greate hart in May — *especially
That in his bed there dawneth him no day

30

That he n'is clad, and ready for to ride
With hunt and horn, and houndes him beside.
For in his hunting hath he such delight,
That it is all his joy and appetite
To be himself the greate harte's bane* *destruction
For after Mars he serveth now Diane.
Clear was the day, as I have told ere this,
And Theseus, with alle joy and bliss,
With his Hippolyta, the faire queen,
And Emily, y-clothed all in green,
On hunting be they ridden royally.
And to the grove, that stood there faste by,
In which there was an hart, as men him told,
Duke Theseus the straighte way doth hold,
And to the laund* he rideth him full right, *plain <33>
There was the hart y-wont to have his flight,
And over a brook, and so forth on his way.
This Duke will have a course at him or tway
With houndes, such as him lust* to command. *pleased
And when this Duke was come to the laund,
Under the sun he looked, and anon
He was ware of Arcite and Palamon,
That foughte breme*, as it were bulles two. *fiercely
The brighte swordes wente to and fro
So hideously, that with the leaste stroke
It seemed that it woulde fell an oak,
But what they were, nothing yet he wote*. *knew
This Duke his courser with his spurres smote,
And at a start he was betwixt them two, *suddenly*
And pulled out a sword and cried, "Ho!
No more, on pain of losing of your head.
By mighty Mars, he shall anon be dead
That smiteth any stroke, that I may see!
But tell to me what mister* men ye be, *manner, kind <34>

That be so hardy for to fighte here
Withoute judge or other officer,
As though it were in listes royally. <35>
This Palamon answered hastily,
And saide: "Sir, what needeth wordes mo'?
We have the death deserved bothe two,
Two woful wretches be we, and caitives,
That be accumbered* of our own lives, *burdened
And as thou art a rightful lord and judge,
So give us neither mercy nor refuge.
And slay me first, for sainte charity,
But slay my fellow eke as well as me.
Or slay him first; for, though thou know it lite*, *little
This is thy mortal foe, this is Arcite
That from thy land is banisht on his head,
For which he hath deserved to be dead.
For this is he that came unto thy gate
And saide, that he highte Philostrate.
Thus hath he japed* thee full many year, *deceived
And thou hast made of him thy chief esquier;
And this is he, that loveth Emily.
For since the day is come that I shall die
I make pleinly* my confession, *fully, unreservedly
That I am thilke* woful Palamon, *that same <36>
That hath thy prison broken wickedly.
I am thy mortal foe, and it am I
That so hot loveth Emily the bright,
That I would die here present in her sight.
Therefore I aske death and my jewise*. *judgement
But slay my fellow eke in the same wise,
For both we have deserved to be slain."

This worthy Duke answer'd anon again,
And said, "This is a short conclusion.

Your own mouth, by your own confession
Hath damned you, and I will it record;
It needeth not to pain you with the cord;
Ye shall be dead, by mighty Mars the Red.<37>

The queen anon for very womanhead
Began to weep, and so did Emily,
And all the ladies in the company.
Great pity was it as it thought them all,
That ever such a chance should befall,
For gentle men they were, of great estate,
And nothing but for love was this debate
They saw their bloody woundes wide and sore,
And cried all at once, both less and more,
"Have mercy, Lord, upon us women all."
And on their bare knees adown they fall
And would have kissed his feet there as he stood,
Till at the last *aslaked was his mood*   *his anger was
(For pity runneth soon in gentle heart); appeased*
And though at first for ire he quoke and start
He hath consider'd shortly in a clause
The trespass of them both, and eke the cause:
And although that his ire their guilt accused
Yet in his reason he them both excused;
As thus; he thoughte well that every man
Will help himself in love if that he can,
And eke deliver himself out of prison.
Of women, for they wepten ever-in-one:*   *continually
And eke his hearte had compassion
And in his gentle heart he thought anon,
And soft unto himself he saide: "Fie
Upon a lord that will have no mercy,
But be a lion both in word and deed,
To them that be in repentance and dread,

33

As well as-to a proud dispiteous* man *unpitying
That will maintaine what he first began.
That lord hath little of discretion,
That in such case *can no division*: *can make no distinction*
But weigheth pride and humbless *after one*." *alike*
And shortly, when his ire is thus agone,
He gan to look on them with eyen light*, *gentle, lenient*
And spake these same wordes *all on height.* *aloud*

"The god of love, ah! benedicite*, *bless ye him
How mighty and how great a lord is he!
Against his might there gaine* none obstacles, *avail, conquer
He may be called a god for his miracles
For he can maken at his owen guise
Of every heart, as that him list devise.
Lo here this Arcite, and this Palamon,
That quietly were out of my prison,
And might have lived in Thebes royally,
And weet* I am their mortal enemy, *knew
And that their death li'th in my might also,
And yet hath love, *maugre their eyen two*, *in spite of their eyes*
Y-brought them hither bothe for to die.
Now look ye, is not this an high folly?
Who may not be a fool, if but he love?
Behold, for Godde's sake that sits above,
See how they bleed! be they not well array'd?
Thus hath their lord, the god of love, them paid
Their wages and their fees for their service;
And yet they weene for to be full wise,
That serve love, for aught that may befall.
But this is yet the beste game* of all, *joke

That she, for whom they have this jealousy,
Can them therefor as muchel thank as me.
She wot no more of all this *hote fare*, *hot behaviour*
By God, than wot a cuckoo or an hare.
But all must be assayed hot or cold;
A man must be a fool, or young or old;
I wot it by myself *full yore agone*: *long years ago*
For in my time a servant was I one.
And therefore since I know of love's pain,
And wot how sore it can a man distrain*, *distress
As he that oft hath been caught in his last*, *snare <38>
I you forgive wholly this trespass,
At request of the queen that kneeleth here,
And eke of Emily, my sister dear.
And ye shall both anon unto me swear,
That never more ye shall my country dere* *injure
Nor make war upon me night nor day,
But be my friends in alle that ye may.
I you forgive this trespass *every deal*. *completely*
And they him sware *his asking* fair and well, *what he
asked*
And him of lordship and of mercy pray'd,
And he them granted grace, and thus he said:

"To speak of royal lineage and richess,
Though that she were a queen or a princess,
Each of you both is worthy doubteless
To wedde when time is; but natheless
I speak as for my sister Emily,
For whom ye have this strife and jealousy,
Ye wot* yourselves, she may not wed the two *know
At once, although ye fight for evermo:
But one of you, *all be him loth or lief,* *whether or not he
wishes*

He must *go pipe into an ivy leaf*: *"go whistle"*
This is to say, she may not have you both,
All be ye never so jealous, nor so wroth.
And therefore I you put in this degree,
That each of you shall have his destiny
As *him is shape*; and hearken in what wise *as is decreed
for him*
Lo hear your end of that I shall devise.
My will is this, for plain conclusion
Withouten any replication*, *reply
If that you liketh, take it for the best,
That evereach of you shall go where *him lest*, *he pleases
Freely without ransom or danger;
And this day fifty weekes, *farre ne nerre*, *neither more
nor less*
Evereach of you shall bring an hundred knights,
Armed for listes up at alle rights
All ready to darraine* her by bataille, *contend for
And this behete* I you withoute fail *promise
Upon my troth, and as I am a knight,
That whether of you bothe that hath might,
That is to say, that whether he or thou
May with his hundred, as I spake of now,
Slay his contrary, or out of listes drive,
Him shall I given Emily to wive,
To whom that fortune gives so fair a grace.
The listes shall I make here in this place.
And God so wisly on my soule rue, *may God as surely
have
As I shall even judge be and true. mercy on my soul*
Ye shall none other ende with me maken
Than one of you shalle be dead or taken.
And if you thinketh this is well y-said,
Say your advice*, and hold yourselves apaid**. *opinion

**satisfied
This is your end, and your conclusion."
Who looketh lightly now but Palamon?
Who springeth up for joye but Arcite?
Who could it tell, or who could it indite,
The joye that is maked in the place
When Theseus hath done so fair a grace?
But down on knees went every *manner wight*, *kind of person*
And thanked him with all their heartes' might,
And namely* these Thebans *ofte sithe*. *especially *oftentimes*
And thus with good hope and with hearte blithe
They take their leave, and homeward gan they ride
To Thebes-ward, with his old walles wide.

I trow men woulde deem it negligence,
If I forgot to telle the dispence* *expenditure
Of Theseus, that went so busily
To maken up the listes royally,
That such a noble theatre as it was,
I dare well say, in all this world there n'as*. *was not
The circuit a mile was about,
Walled of stone, and ditched all without.
*Round was the shape, in manner of compass,
Full of degrees, the height of sixty pas* *see note <39>*
That when a man was set on one degree
He letted* not his fellow for to see. *hindered
Eastward there stood a gate of marble white,
Westward right such another opposite.
And, shortly to conclude, such a place
Was never on earth made in so little space,
For in the land there was no craftes-man,
That geometry or arsmetrike* can**, *arithmetic **knew

Nor pourtrayor*, nor carver of images, *portrait painter
That Theseus ne gave him meat and wages
The theatre to make and to devise.
And for to do his rite and sacrifice
He eastward hath upon the gate above,
In worship of Venus, goddess of love,
Done make an altar and an oratory; *caused to be made*
And westward, in the mind and in memory
Of Mars, he maked hath right such another,
That coste largely of gold a fother*. *a great amount
And northward, in a turret on the wall,
Of alabaster white and red coral
An oratory riche for to see,
In worship of Diane of chastity,
Hath Theseus done work in noble wise.
But yet had I forgotten to devise* *describe
The noble carving, and the portraitures,
The shape, the countenance of the figures
That weren in there oratories three.

First in the temple of Venus may'st thou see
Wrought on the wall, full piteous to behold,
The broken sleepes, and the sikes* cold, *sighes
The sacred teares, and the waimentings*, *lamentings
The fiery strokes of the desirings,
That Love's servants in this life endure;
The oathes, that their covenants assure.
Pleasance and Hope, Desire, Foolhardiness,
Beauty and Youth, and Bawdry and Richess,
Charms and Sorc'ry, Leasings* and Flattery, *falsehoods
Dispence, Business, and Jealousy,
That wore of yellow goldes* a garland, *sunflowers <40>
And had a cuckoo sitting on her hand,
Feasts, instruments, and caroles and dances,

38

Lust and array, and all the circumstances
Of Love, which I reckon'd and reckon shall
In order, were painted on the wall,
And more than I can make of mention.
For soothly all the mount of Citheron,<41>
Where Venus hath her principal dwelling,
Was showed on the wall in pourtraying,
With all the garden, and the lustiness*. *pleasantness
Nor was forgot the porter Idleness,
Nor Narcissus the fair of *yore agone*, *olden times*
Nor yet the folly of King Solomon,
Nor yet the greate strength of Hercules,
Th' enchantments of Medea and Circes,
Nor of Turnus the hardy fierce courage,
The rich Croesus *caitif in servage.* <42> *abased into
slavery*
Thus may ye see, that wisdom nor richess,
Beauty, nor sleight, nor strength, nor hardiness
Ne may with Venus holde champartie*, *divided possession
<43>
For as her liste the world may she gie*. *guide
Lo, all these folk so caught were in her las* *snare
Till they for woe full often said, Alas!
Suffice these ensamples one or two,
Although I could reckon a thousand mo'.

The statue of Venus, glorious to see
Was naked floating in the large sea,
And from the navel down all cover'd was
With waves green, and bright as any glass.
A citole <44> in her right hand hadde she,
And on her head, full seemly for to see,
A rose garland fresh, and well smelling,
Above her head her doves flickering

Before her stood her sone Cupido,
Upon his shoulders winges had he two;
And blind he was, as it is often seen;
A bow he bare, and arrows bright and keen.

Why should I not as well eke tell you all
The portraiture, that was upon the wall
Within the temple of mighty Mars the Red?
All painted was the wall in length and brede* *breadth
Like to the estres* of the grisly place *interior chambers
That hight the great temple of Mars in Thrace,
In thilke* cold and frosty region, *that
There as Mars hath his sovereign mansion.
In which there dwelled neither man nor beast,
With knotty gnarry* barren trees old *gnarled
Of stubbes sharp and hideous to behold;
In which there ran a rumble and a sough*, *groaning noise
As though a storm should bursten every bough:
And downward from an hill under a bent* *slope
There stood the temple of Mars Armipotent,
Wrought all of burnish'd steel, of which th' entry
Was long and strait, and ghastly for to see.
And thereout came *a rage and such a vise*, *such a furious
voice*
That it made all the gates for to rise.
The northern light in at the doore shone,
For window on the walle was there none
Through which men mighten any light discern.
The doors were all of adamant etern,
Y-clenched *overthwart and ende-long* *crossways and
lengthways*
With iron tough, and, for to make it strong,
Every pillar the temple to sustain
Was tunne-great*, of iron bright and sheen. *thick as a tun

40

(barrel)
There saw I first the dark imagining
Of felony, and all the compassing;
The cruel ire, as red as any glede*, *live coal
The picke-purse<45>, and eke the pale dread;
The smiler with the knife under the cloak,
The shepen* burning with the blacke smoke *stable <46>
The treason of the murd'ring in the bed,
The open war, with woundes all be-bled;
Conteke* with bloody knife, and sharp menace. *contention,
discord
All full of chirking* was that sorry place. *creaking, jarring
noise
The slayer of himself eke saw I there,
His hearte-blood had bathed all his hair:
The nail y-driven in the shode* at night, *hair of the head
<47>
The colde death, with mouth gaping upright.
Amiddes of the temple sat Mischance,
With discomfort and sorry countenance;
Eke saw I Woodness* laughing in his rage, *Madness
Armed Complaint, Outhees*, and fierce Outrage; *Outcry
The carrain* in the bush, with throat y-corve**, *corpse
**slashed
A thousand slain, and not *of qualm y-storve*; *dead of
sickness*
The tyrant, with the prey by force y-reft;
The town destroy'd, that there was nothing left.
Yet saw I brent* the shippes hoppesteres, <48> *burnt
The hunter strangled with the wilde bears:
The sow freting* the child right in the cradle; *devouring
<49>
The cook scalded, for all his longe ladle.
Nor was forgot, *by th'infortune of Mart* *through the

misfortune
The carter overridden with his cart; of war*
Under the wheel full low he lay adown.
There were also of Mars' division,
The armourer, the bowyer*, and the smith, *maker of bows
That forgeth sharp swordes on his stith*. *anvil
And all above depainted in a tower
Saw I Conquest, sitting in great honour,
With thilke* sharpe sword over his head *that
Hanging by a subtle y-twined thread.
Painted the slaughter was of Julius<50>,
Of cruel Nero, and Antonius:
Although at that time they were yet unborn,
Yet was their death depainted there beforn,
By menacing of Mars, right by figure,
So was it showed in that portraiture,
As is depainted in the stars above,
Who shall be slain, or elles dead for love.
Sufficeth one ensample in stories old,
I may not reckon them all, though I wo'ld.

The statue of Mars upon a carte* stood *chariot
Armed, and looked grim as he were wood*, *mad
And over his head there shone two figures
Of starres, that be cleped in scriptures,
That one Puella, that other Rubeus. <51>
This god of armes was arrayed thus:
A wolf there stood before him at his feet
With eyen red, and of a man he eat:
With subtle pencil painted was this story,
In redouting* of Mars and of his glory. *reverance, fear

Now to the temple of Dian the chaste
As shortly as I can I will me haste,

To telle you all the descriptioun.
Depainted be the walles up and down
Of hunting and of shamefast chastity.
There saw I how woful Calistope,<52>
When that Dian aggrieved was with her,
Was turned from a woman to a bear,
And after was she made the lodestar*: *pole star
Thus was it painted, I can say no far*; *farther
Her son is eke a star as men may see.
There saw I Dane <53> turn'd into a tree,
I meane not the goddess Diane,
But Peneus' daughter, which that hight Dane.
There saw I Actaeon an hart y-maked*, *made
For vengeance that he saw Dian all naked:
I saw how that his houndes have him caught,
And freten* him, for that they knew him not. *devour
Yet painted was, a little farthermore
How Atalanta hunted the wild boar;
And Meleager, and many other mo',
For which Diana wrought them care and woe.
There saw I many another wondrous story,
The which me list not drawen to memory.
This goddess on an hart full high was set*, *seated
With smalle houndes all about her feet,
And underneath her feet she had a moon,
Waxing it was, and shoulde wane soon.
In gaudy green her statue clothed was,
With bow in hand, and arrows in a case*. *quiver
Her eyen caste she full low adown,
Where Pluto hath his darke regioun.
A woman travailing was her beforn,
But, for her child so longe was unborn,
Full piteously Lucina <54> gan she call,
And saide; "Help, for thou may'st best of all."

Well could he painte lifelike that it wrought;
With many a florin he the hues had bought.
Now be these listes made, and Theseus,
That at his greate cost arrayed thus
The temples, and the theatre every deal*, *part <55>
When it was done, him liked wonder well.

But stint* I will of Theseus a lite**, *cease speaking **little
And speak of Palamon and of Arcite.
The day approacheth of their returning,
That evereach an hundred knights should bring,
The battle to darraine* as I you told; *contest
And to Athens, their covenant to hold,
Hath ev'reach of them brought an hundred knights,
Well-armed for the war at alle rights.
And sickerly* there trowed** many a man, *surely <56>
**believed
That never, sithen* that the world began, *since
For to speaken of knighthood of their hand,
As far as God hath maked sea and land,
Was, of so few, so noble a company.
For every wight that loved chivalry,
And would, *his thankes, have a passant name*, *thanks to
his own
Had prayed, that he might be of that game, efforts, have a
And well was him, that thereto chosen was. surpassing
name*
For if there fell to-morrow such a case,
Ye knowe well, that every lusty knight,
That loveth par amour, and hath his might
Were it in Engleland, or elleswhere,
They would, their thankes, willen to be there,
T' fight for a lady; Benedicite,
It were a lusty* sighte for to see. *pleasing

And right so fared they with Palamon;
With him there wente knightes many one.
Some will be armed in an habergeon,
And in a breast-plate, and in a gipon*; *short doublet.
And some will have *a pair of plates* large; *back and front
armour*
And some will have a Prusse* shield, or targe; *Prussian
Some will be armed on their legges weel;
Some have an axe, and some a mace of steel.
There is no newe guise*, but it was old. *fashion
Armed they weren, as I have you told,
Evereach after his opinion.
There may'st thou see coming with Palamon
Licurgus himself, the great king of Thrace:
Black was his beard, and manly was his face.
The circles of his eyen in his head
They glowed betwixte yellow and red,
And like a griffin looked he about,
With kemped* haires on his browes stout; *combed<57>
His limbs were great, his brawns were hard and strong,
His shoulders broad, his armes round and long.
And as the guise* was in his country, *fashion
Full high upon a car of gold stood he,
With foure white bulles in the trace.
Instead of coat-armour on his harness,
With yellow nails, and bright as any gold,
He had a beare's skin, coal-black for old*. *age
His long hair was y-kempt behind his back,
As any raven's feather it shone for black.
A wreath of gold *arm-great*, of huge weight, *thick as a
man's arm*
Upon his head sate, full of stones bright,
Of fine rubies and clear diamants.
About his car there wente white alauns*, *greyhounds <58>

Twenty and more, as great as any steer,
To hunt the lion or the wilde bear,
And follow'd him, with muzzle fast y-bound,
Collars of gold, and torettes* filed round. *rings
An hundred lordes had he in his rout* *retinue
Armed full well, with heartes stern and stout.

With Arcita, in stories as men find,
The great Emetrius the king of Ind,
Upon a *steede bay* trapped in steel, *bay horse*
Cover'd with cloth of gold diapred* well, *decorated
Came riding like the god of armes, Mars.
His coat-armour was of *a cloth of Tars*, *a kind of silk*
Couched* with pearls white and round and great *trimmed
His saddle was of burnish'd gold new beat;
A mantelet on his shoulders hanging,
Bretful* of rubies red, as fire sparkling. *brimful
His crispe hair like ringes was y-run,
And that was yellow, glittering as the sun.
His nose was high, his eyen bright citrine*, *pale yellow
His lips were round, his colour was sanguine,
A fewe fracknes* in his face y-sprent**, *freckles
**sprinkled
Betwixte yellow and black somedeal y-ment* *mixed <59>
And as a lion he *his looking cast* *cast about his eyes*
Of five and twenty year his age I cast* *reckon
His beard was well begunnen for to spring;
His voice was as a trumpet thundering.
Upon his head he wore of laurel green
A garland fresh and lusty to be seen;
Upon his hand he bare, for his delight,
An eagle tame, as any lily white.
An hundred lordes had he with him there,
All armed, save their heads, in all their gear,

46

Full richely in alle manner things.
For trust ye well, that earles, dukes, and kings
Were gather'd in this noble company,
For love, and for increase of chivalry.
About this king there ran on every part
Full many a tame lion and leopart.
And in this wise these lordes *all and some* *all and
sundry*
Be on the Sunday to the city come
Aboute prime<60>, and in the town alight.

This Theseus, this Duke, this worthy knight
When he had brought them into his city,
And inned* them, ev'reach at his degree, *lodged
He feasteth them, and doth so great labour
To *easen them*, and do them all honour, *make them
comfortable*
That yet men weene* that no mannes wit *think
Of none estate could amenden* it. *improve
The minstrelsy, the service at the feast,
The greate giftes to the most and least,
The rich array of Theseus' palace,
Nor who sate first or last upon the dais.<61>
What ladies fairest be, or best dancing
Or which of them can carol best or sing,
Or who most feelingly speaketh of love;
What hawkes sitten on the perch above,
What houndes liggen* on the floor adown, *lie
Of all this now make I no mentioun
But of th'effect; that thinketh me the best
Now comes the point, and hearken if you lest.* *please

The Sunday night, ere day began to spring,
When Palamon the larke hearde sing,

47

Although it were not day by houres two,
Yet sang the lark, and Palamon right tho* *then
With holy heart, and with an high courage,
Arose, to wenden* on his pilgrimage *go
Unto the blissful Cithera benign,
I meane Venus, honourable and digne*. *worthy
And in her hour <62> he walketh forth a pace
Unto the listes, where her temple was,
And down he kneeleth, and with humble cheer* *demeanour
And hearte sore, he said as ye shall hear.

"Fairest of fair, O lady mine Venus,
Daughter to Jove, and spouse of Vulcanus,
Thou gladder of the mount of Citheron!<41>
For thilke love thou haddest to Adon <63>
Have pity on my bitter teares smart,
And take mine humble prayer to thine heart.
Alas! I have no language to tell
Th'effecte, nor the torment of mine hell;
Mine hearte may mine harmes not betray;
I am so confused, that I cannot say.
But mercy, lady bright, that knowest well
My thought, and seest what harm that I feel.
Consider all this, and *rue upon* my sore, *take pity on*
As wisly* as I shall for evermore *truly
Enforce my might, thy true servant to be,
And holde war alway with chastity:
That make I mine avow*, so ye me help. *vow, promise
I keepe not of armes for to yelp,* *boast
Nor ask I not to-morrow to have victory,
Nor renown in this case, nor vaine glory
Of *prize of armes*, blowing up and down, *praise for
valour*
But I would have fully possessioun

48

Of Emily, and die in her service;
Find thou the manner how, and in what wise.
I *recke not but* it may better be *do not know whether*
To have vict'ry of them, or they of me,
So that I have my lady in mine arms.
For though so be that Mars is god of arms,
Your virtue is so great in heaven above,
That, if you list, I shall well have my love.
Thy temple will I worship evermo',
And on thine altar, where I ride or go,
I will do sacrifice, and fires bete*. *make, kindle
And if ye will not so, my lady sweet,
Then pray I you, to-morrow with a spear
That Arcita me through the hearte bear
Then reck I not, when I have lost my life,
Though that Arcita win her to his wife.
This is th' effect and end of my prayere, —
Give me my love, thou blissful lady dear."
When th' orison was done of Palamon,
His sacrifice he did, and that anon,
Full piteously, with alle circumstances,
All tell I not as now his observances. *although I tell not
now*
But at the last the statue of Venus shook,
And made a signe, whereby that he took
That his prayer accepted was that day.
For though the signe shewed a delay,
Yet wist he well that granted was his boon;
And with glad heart he went him home full soon.

The third hour unequal <64> that Palamon
Began to Venus' temple for to gon,
Up rose the sun, and up rose Emily,
And to the temple of Dian gan hie.

Her maidens, that she thither with her lad*, *led
Th' incense, the clothes, and the remnant all
That to the sacrifice belonge shall,
The hornes full of mead, as was the guise;
There lacked nought to do her sacrifice.
Smoking* the temple full of clothes fair, *draping <65>
This Emily with hearte debonnair* *gentle
Her body wash'd with water of a well.
But how she did her rite I dare not tell;
But* it be any thing in general; *unless
And yet it were a game* to hearen all *pleasure
To him that meaneth well it were no charge:
But it is good a man to *be at large*. *do as he will*
Her bright hair combed was, untressed all.
A coronet of green oak cerriall <66>
Upon her head was set full fair and meet.
Two fires on the altar gan she bete,
And did her thinges, as men may behold
In Stace of Thebes <67>, and these bookes old.
When kindled was the fire, with piteous cheer
Unto Dian she spake as ye may hear.

"O chaste goddess of the woodes green,
To whom both heav'n and earth and sea is seen,
Queen of the realm of Pluto dark and low,
Goddess of maidens, that mine heart hast know
Full many a year, and wost* what I desire, *knowest
To keep me from the vengeance of thine ire,
That Actaeon aboughte* cruelly: *earned; suffered from
Chaste goddess, well wottest thou that I
Desire to be a maiden all my life,
Nor never will I be no love nor wife.
I am, thou wost*, yet of thy company, *knowest
A maid, and love hunting and venery*, *field sports

50

And for to walken in the woodes wild,
And not to be a wife, and be with child.
Nought will I know the company of man.
Now help me, lady, since ye may and can,
For those three formes <68> that thou hast in thee.
And Palamon, that hath such love to me,
And eke Arcite, that loveth me so sore,
This grace I pray thee withoute more,
As sende love and peace betwixt them two:
And from me turn away their heartes so,
That all their hote love, and their desire,
And all their busy torment, and their fire,
Be queint*, or turn'd into another place. *quenched
And if so be thou wilt do me no grace,
Or if my destiny be shapen so
That I shall needes have one of them two,
So send me him that most desireth me.
Behold, goddess of cleane chastity,
The bitter tears that on my cheekes fall.
Since thou art maid, and keeper of us all,
My maidenhead thou keep and well conserve,
And, while I live, a maid I will thee serve.

The fires burn upon the altar clear,
While Emily was thus in her prayere:
But suddenly she saw a sighte quaint*. *strange
For right anon one of the fire's *queint
And quick'd* again, and after that anon *went out and
revived*
That other fire was queint, and all agone:
And as it queint, it made a whisteling,
As doth a brande wet in its burning.
And at the brandes end outran anon
As it were bloody droppes many one:

51

For which so sore aghast was Emily,
That she was well-nigh mad, and gan to cry,
For she ne wiste what it signified;
But onely for feare thus she cried,
And wept, that it was pity for to hear.
And therewithal Diana gan appear
With bow in hand, right as an hunteress,
And saide; "Daughter, stint* thine heaviness. *cease
Among the goddes high it is affirm'd,
And by eternal word writ and confirm'd,
Thou shalt be wedded unto one of tho* *those
That have for thee so muche care and woe:
But unto which of them I may not tell.
Farewell, for here I may no longer dwell.
The fires which that on mine altar brenn*, *burn
Shall thee declaren, ere that thou go henne*, *hence
Thine aventure of love, as in this case."
And with that word, the arrows in the case* *quiver
Of the goddess did clatter fast and ring,
And forth she went, and made a vanishing,
For which this Emily astonied was,
And saide; "What amounteth this, alas!
I put me under thy protection,
Diane, and in thy disposition."
And home she went anon the nexte* way. *nearest
This is th' effect, there is no more to say.

The nexte hour of Mars following this
Arcite to the temple walked is
Of fierce Mars, to do his sacrifice
With all the rites of his pagan guise.
With piteous* heart and high devotion *pious
Right thus to Mars he said his orison
"O stronge god, that in the regnes* old *realms

52

Of Thrace honoured art, and lord y-hold* *held
And hast in every regne, and every land
Of armes all the bridle in thine hand,
And *them fortunest as thee list devise*, *send them fortune
Accept of me my piteous sacrifice. as you please*
If so be that my youthe may deserve,
And that my might be worthy for to serve
Thy godhead, that I may be one of thine,
Then pray I thee to *rue upon my pine*, *pity my anguish*
For thilke* pain, and thilke hote fire, *that
In which thou whilom burned'st for desire
Whenne that thou usedest* the beauty *enjoyed
Of faire young Venus, fresh and free,
And haddest her in armes at thy will:
And though thee ones on a time misfill*, *were unlucky
When Vulcanus had caught thee in his las*, *net <69>
And found thee ligging* by his wife, alas! *lying
For thilke sorrow that was in thine heart,
Have ruth* as well upon my paine's smart. *pity
I am young and unconning*, as thou know'st, *ignorant,
simple
And, as I trow*, with love offended most *believe
That e'er was any living creature:
For she, that doth* me all this woe endure, *causes
Ne recketh ne'er whether I sink or fleet* *swim
And well I wot, ere she me mercy hete*, *promise,
vouchsafe
I must with strengthe win her in the place:
And well I wot, withoute help or grace
Of thee, ne may my strengthe not avail:
Then help me, lord, to-morr'w in my bataille,
For thilke fire that whilom burned thee,
As well as this fire that now burneth me;
And do* that I to-morr'w may have victory. *cause

Mine be the travail, all thine be the glory.
Thy sovereign temple will I most honour
Of any place, and alway most labour
In thy pleasance and in thy craftes strong.
And in thy temple I will my banner hong*, *hang
And all the armes of my company,
And evermore, until that day I die,
Eternal fire I will before thee find
And eke to this my vow I will me bind:
My beard, my hair that hangeth long adown,
That never yet hath felt offension* *indignity
Of razor nor of shears, I will thee give,
And be thy true servant while I live.
Now, lord, have ruth upon my sorrows sore,
Give me the victory, I ask no more."

The prayer stint* of Arcita the strong, *ended
The ringes on the temple door that hong,
And eke the doores, clattered full fast,
Of which Arcita somewhat was aghast.
The fires burn'd upon the altar bright,
That it gan all the temple for to light;
A sweete smell anon the ground up gaf*, *gave
And Arcita anon his hand up haf*, *lifted
And more incense into the fire he cast,
With other rites more and at the last
The statue of Mars began his hauberk ring;
And with that sound he heard a murmuring
Full low and dim, that saide thus, "Victory."
For which he gave to Mars honour and glory.
And thus with joy, and hope well to fare,
Arcite anon unto his inn doth fare.
As fain* as fowl is of the brighte sun. *glad

And right anon such strife there is begun
For thilke* granting, in the heav'n above, *that
Betwixte Venus the goddess of love,
And Mars the sterne god armipotent,
That Jupiter was busy it to stent*: *stop
Till that the pale Saturnus the cold,<70>
That knew so many of adventures old,
Found in his old experience such an art,
That he full soon hath pleased every part.
As sooth is said, eld* hath great advantage, *age
In eld is bothe wisdom and usage*: *experience
Men may the old out-run, but not out-rede*. *outwit
Saturn anon, to stint the strife and drede,
Albeit that it is against his kind,* *nature
Of all this strife gan a remedy find.
"My deare daughter Venus," quoth Saturn,
"My course*, that hath so wide for to turn, *orbit <71>
Hath more power than wot any man.
Mine is the drowning in the sea so wan;
Mine is the prison in the darke cote*, *cell
Mine the strangling and hanging by the throat,
The murmur, and the churlish rebelling,
The groyning*, and the privy poisoning. *discontent
I do vengeance and plein* correction, *full
I dwell in the sign of the lion.
Mine is the ruin of the highe halls,
The falling of the towers and the walls
Upon the miner or the carpenter:
I slew Samson in shaking the pillar:
Mine also be the maladies cold,
The darke treasons, and the castes* old: *plots
My looking is the father of pestilence.
Now weep no more, I shall do diligence
That Palamon, that is thine owen knight,

Shall have his lady, as thou hast him hight*. *promised
Though Mars shall help his knight, yet natheless
Betwixte you there must sometime be peace:
All be ye not of one complexion,
That each day causeth such division,
I am thine ayel*, ready at thy will; *grandfather <72>
Weep now no more, I shall thy lust* fulfil." *pleasure
Now will I stenten* of the gods above, *cease speaking
Of Mars, and of Venus, goddess of love,
And telle you as plainly as I can
The great effect, for which that I began.

Great was the feast in Athens thilke* day; *that
And eke the lusty season of that May
Made every wight to be in such pleasance,
That all that Monday jousten they and dance,
And spenden it in Venus' high service.
But by the cause that they shoulde rise
Early a-morrow for to see that fight,
Unto their reste wente they at night.
And on the morrow, when the day gan spring,
Of horse and harness* noise and clattering *armour
There was in the hostelries all about:
And to the palace rode there many a rout* *train, retinue
Of lordes, upon steedes and palfreys.
There mayst thou see devising* of harness *decoration
So uncouth* and so rich, and wrought so weel *unkown, rare
Of goldsmithry, of brouding*, and of steel; *embroidery
The shieldes bright, the testers*, and trappures**
*helmets<73>
Gold-hewen helmets, hauberks, coat-armures; **trappings
Lordes in parements* on their coursers, *ornamental garb
<74>;
Knightes of retinue, and eke squiers,

56

Nailing the spears, and helmes buckeling,
Gniding* of shieldes, with lainers** lacing; *polishing <75>
There as need is, they were nothing idle: **lanyards
The foamy steeds upon the golden bridle
Gnawing, and fast the armourers also
With file and hammer pricking to and fro;
Yeomen on foot, and knaves* many one *servants
With shorte staves, thick* as they may gon**; *close **walk
Pipes, trumpets, nakeres*, and clariouns, *drums <76>
That in the battle blowe bloody souns;
The palace full of people up and down,
There three, there ten, holding their questioun*,
*conversation
Divining* of these Theban knightes two. *conjecturing
Some saiden thus, some said it shall he so;
Some helden with him with the blacke beard,
Some with the bald, some with the thick-hair'd;
Some said he looked grim, and woulde fight:
He had a sparth* of twenty pound of weight. *double-headed
axe
Thus was the halle full of divining* *conjecturing
Long after that the sunne gan up spring.
The great Theseus that of his sleep is waked
With minstrelsy, and noise that was maked,
Held yet the chamber of his palace rich,
Till that the Theban knightes both y-lich* *alike
Honoured were, and to the palace fet*. *fetched
Duke Theseus is at a window set,
Array'd right as he were a god in throne:
The people presseth thitherward full soon
Him for to see, and do him reverence,
And eke to hearken his hest* and his sentence**. *command
**speech
An herald on a scaffold made an O, <77>

Till the noise of the people was y-do*: *done
And when he saw the people of noise all still,
Thus shewed he the mighty Duke's will.
"The lord hath of his high discretion
Considered that it were destruction
To gentle blood, to fighten in the guise
Of mortal battle now in this emprise:
Wherefore to shape* that they shall not die, *arrange,
contrive
He will his firste purpose modify.
No man therefore, on pain of loss of life,
No manner* shot, nor poleaxe, nor short knife *kind of
Into the lists shall send, or thither bring.
Nor short sword for to stick with point biting
No man shall draw, nor bear it by his side.
And no man shall unto his fellow ride
But one course, with a sharp y-grounden spear:
*Foin if him list on foot, himself to wear. *He who wishes
can
And he that is at mischief shall be take*, fence on foot to
defend
And not slain, but be brought unto the stake, himself, and he
that
That shall be ordained on either side; is in peril shall be
taken*
Thither he shall by force, and there abide.
And if *so fall* the chiefetain be take *should happen*
On either side, or elles slay his make*, *equal, match
No longer then the tourneying shall last.
God speede you; go forth and lay on fast.
With long sword and with mace fight your fill.
Go now your way; this is the lordes will.
The voice of the people touched the heaven,
So loude cried they with merry steven*: *sound

God save such a lord that is so good,
He willeth no destruction of blood.

Up go the trumpets and the melody,
And to the listes rode the company
By ordinance, throughout the city large, *in orderly array*
Hanged with cloth of gold, and not with sarge*. *serge <78>
Full like a lord this noble Duke gan ride,
And these two Thebans upon either side:

And after rode the queen and Emily,
And after them another company
Of one and other, after their degree.
And thus they passed thorough that city
And to the listes came they by time:
It was not of the day yet fully prime*. *between 6 & 9 a.m.
When set was Theseus full rich and high,
Hippolyta the queen and Emily,
And other ladies in their degrees about,
Unto the seates presseth all the rout.
And westward, through the gates under Mart,
Arcite, and eke the hundred of his part,
With banner red, is enter'd right anon;
And in the selve* moment Palamon *self-same
Is, under Venus, eastward in the place,
With banner white, and hardy cheer* and face *expression
In all the world, to seeken up and down
So even* without variatioun *equal
There were such companies never tway.
For there was none so wise that coulde say
That any had of other avantage
Of worthiness, nor of estate, nor age,
So even were they chosen for to guess.
And *in two ranges faire they them dress*. *they arranged

themselves

When that their names read were every one, in two rows*

That in their number guile* were there none, *fraud

Then were the gates shut, and cried was loud;

"Do now your devoir, younge knights proud

The heralds left their pricking* up and down *spurring their horses

Now ring the trumpet loud and clarioun.

There is no more to say, but east and west

In go the speares sadly* in the rest; *steadily

In go the sharpe spurs into the side.

There see me who can joust, and who can ride.

There shiver shaftes upon shieldes thick;

He feeleth through the hearte-spoon<79> the prick.

Up spring the speares twenty foot on height;

Out go the swordes as the silver bright.

The helmes they to-hewen, and to-shred*; *strike in pieces <80>

Out burst the blood, with sterne streames red.

With mighty maces the bones they to-brest*. *burst

He <81> through the thickest of the throng gan threst*. *thrust

There stumble steedes strong, and down go all.

He rolleth under foot as doth a ball.

He foineth* on his foe with a trunchoun, *forces himself

And he him hurtleth with his horse adown.

He through the body hurt is, and *sith take*, *afterwards captured*

Maugre his head, and brought unto the stake,

As forword* was, right there he must abide. *covenant

Another led is on that other side.

And sometime doth* them Theseus to rest, *caused

Them to refresh, and drinken if them lest*. *pleased

Full oft a day have thilke Thebans two *these

Together met and wrought each other woe:
Unhorsed hath each other of them tway* *twice
There is no tiger in the vale of Galaphay, <82>
When that her whelp is stole, when it is lite* *little
So cruel on the hunter, as Arcite
For jealous heart upon this Palamon:
Nor in Belmarie <83> there is no fell lion,
That hunted is, or for his hunger wood* *mad
Or for his prey desireth so the blood,
As Palamon to slay his foe Arcite.
The jealous strokes upon their helmets bite;
Out runneth blood on both their sides red,
Sometime an end there is of every deed
For ere the sun unto the reste went,
The stronge king Emetrius gan hent* *sieze, assail
This Palamon, as he fought with Arcite,
And made his sword deep in his flesh to bite,
And by the force of twenty is he take,
Unyielding, and is drawn unto the stake.
And in the rescue of this Palamon
The stronge king Licurgus is borne down:
And king Emetrius, for all his strength
Is borne out of his saddle a sword's length,
So hit him Palamon ere he were take:
But all for nought; he was brought to the stake:
His hardy hearte might him helpe naught,
He must abide when that he was caught,
By force, and eke by composition*. *the bargain
Who sorroweth now but woful Palamon
That must no more go again to fight?
And when that Theseus had seen that sight
Unto the folk that foughte thus each one,
He cried, Ho! no more, for it is done!
I will be true judge, and not party.

Arcite of Thebes shall have Emily,
That by his fortune hath her fairly won."
Anon there is a noise of people gone,
For joy of this, so loud and high withal,
It seemed that the listes shoulde fall.

What can now faire Venus do above?
What saith she now? what doth this queen of love?
But weepeth so, for wanting of her will,
Till that her teares in the listes fill* *fall
She said: "I am ashamed doubteless."
Saturnus saide: "Daughter, hold thy peace.
Mars hath his will, his knight hath all his boon,
And by mine head thou shalt be eased soon."
 The trumpeters with the loud minstrelsy,
The heralds, that full loude yell and cry,
Be in their joy for weal of Dan* Arcite. *Lord
But hearken me, and stinte noise a lite,
What a miracle there befell anon
This fierce Arcite hath off his helm y-done,
And on a courser for to shew his face
He *pricketh endelong* the large place, *rides from end to end*
Looking upward upon this Emily;
And she again him cast a friendly eye
(For women, as to speaken *in commune*, *generally*
They follow all the favour of fortune),
And was all his in cheer*, as his in heart. *countenance
Out of the ground a fire infernal start,
From Pluto sent, at request of Saturn
For which his horse for fear began to turn,
And leap aside, and founder* as he leap *stumble
And ere that Arcite may take any keep*, *care
He pight* him on the pummel** of his head. *pitched **top

62

That in the place he lay as he were dead.
His breast to-bursten with his saddle-bow.
As black he lay as any coal or crow,
So was the blood y-run into his face.
Anon he was y-borne out of the place
With hearte sore, to Theseus' palace.
Then was he carven* out of his harness. *cut
And in a bed y-brought full fair and blive* *quickly
For he was yet in mem'ry and alive,
And always crying after Emily.

Duke Theseus, with all his company,
Is come home to Athens his city,
With alle bliss and great solemnity.
Albeit that this aventure was fall*, *befallen
He woulde not discomforte* them all *discourage
Then said eke, that Arcite should not die,
He should be healed of his malady.
And of another thing they were as fain*. *glad
That of them alle was there no one slain,
All* were they sorely hurt, and namely** one, *although
**especially
That with a spear was thirled* his breast-bone. *pierced
To other woundes, and to broken arms,
Some hadden salves, and some hadden charms:
And pharmacies of herbs, and eke save* *sage, Salvia
officinalis
They dranken, for they would their lives have.
For which this noble Duke, as he well can,
Comforteth and honoureth every man,
And made revel all the longe night,
Unto the strange lordes, as was right.
Nor there was holden no discomforting,
But as at jousts or at a tourneying;

For soothly there was no discomfiture,
For falling is not but an aventure*. *chance, accident
Nor to be led by force unto a stake
Unyielding, and with twenty knights y-take
One person all alone, withouten mo',
And harried* forth by armes, foot, and toe, *dragged, hurried
And eke his steede driven forth with staves,
With footmen, bothe yeomen and eke knaves*, *servants
It was *aretted him no villainy:* *counted no disgrace to
him*
There may no man *clepen it cowardy*. *call it cowardice*
For which anon Duke Theseus *let cry*, — *caused to be
proclaimed*
To stenten* alle rancour and envy, — *stop
The gree* as well on one side as the other, *prize, merit
And either side alike as other's brother:
And gave them giftes after their degree,
And held a feaste fully dayes three:
And conveyed the kinges worthily
Out of his town a journee* largely *day's journey
And home went every man the righte way,
There was no more but "Farewell, Have good day."
Of this bataille I will no more indite
But speak of Palamon and of Arcite.

Swelleth the breast of Arcite and the sore
Increaseth at his hearte more and more.
The clotted blood, for any leache-craft* *surgical skill
Corrupteth and is *in his bouk y-laft* *left in his body*
That neither *veine blood nor ventousing*, *blood-letting or
cupping*
Nor drink of herbes may be his helping.
The virtue expulsive or animal,
From thilke virtue called natural,

Nor may the venom voide, nor expel
The pipes of his lungs began to swell
And every lacert* in his breast adown *sinew, muscle
Is shent* with venom and corruption. *destroyed
Him gaineth* neither, for to get his life, *availeth
Vomit upward, nor downward laxative;
All is to-bursten thilke region;
Nature hath now no domination.
And certainly where nature will not wirch,* *work
Farewell physic: go bear the man to chirch.* *church
This all and some is, Arcite must die.
For which he sendeth after Emily,
And Palamon, that was his cousin dear,
Then said he thus, as ye shall after hear.

"Nought may the woful spirit in mine heart
Declare one point of all my sorrows' smart
To you, my lady, that I love the most:
But I bequeath the service of my ghost
To you aboven every creature,
Since that my life ne may no longer dure.
Alas the woe! alas, the paines strong
That I for you have suffered and so long!
Alas the death, alas, mine Emily!
Alas departing* of our company! *the severance
Alas, mine hearte's queen! alas, my wife!
Mine hearte's lady, ender of my life!
What is this world? what aske men to have?
Now with his love, now in his colde grave
Al one, withouten any company.
Farewell, my sweet, farewell, mine Emily,
And softly take me in your armes tway,
For love of God, and hearken what I say.
I have here with my cousin Palamon

Had strife and rancour many a day agone,
For love of you, and for my jealousy.
And Jupiter so *wis my soule gie*, *surely guides my soul*
To speaken of a servant properly,
With alle circumstances truely,
That is to say, truth, honour, and knighthead,
Wisdom, humbless*, estate, and high kindred, *humility
Freedom, and all that longeth to that art,
So Jupiter have of my soul part,
As in this world right now I know not one,
So worthy to be lov'd as Palamon,
That serveth you, and will do all his life.
And if that you shall ever be a wife,
Forget not Palamon, the gentle man."

And with that word his speech to fail began.
For from his feet up to his breast was come
The cold of death, that had him overnome*. *overcome
And yet moreover in his armes two
The vital strength is lost, and all ago*. *gone
Only the intellect, withoute more,
That dwelled in his hearte sick and sore,
Gan faile, when the hearte felte death;
Dusked* his eyen two, and fail'd his breath. *grew dim
But on his lady yet he cast his eye;
His laste word was; "Mercy, Emily!"
His spirit changed house, and wente there,
As I came never I cannot telle where.<84>
Therefore I stent*, I am no divinister**; *refrain **diviner
Of soules find I nought in this register.
Ne me list not th' opinions to tell
Of them, though that they writen where they dwell;
Arcite is cold, there Mars his soule gie.* *guide
Now will I speake forth of Emily.

Shriek'd Emily, and howled Palamon,
And Theseus his sister took anon
Swooning, and bare her from the corpse away.
What helpeth it to tarry forth the day,
To telle how she wept both eve and morrow?
For in such cases women have such sorrow,
When that their husbands be from them y-go*, *gone
That for the more part they sorrow so,
Or elles fall into such malady,
That at the laste certainly they die.
Infinite be the sorrows and the tears
Of olde folk, and folk of tender years,
In all the town, for death of this Theban:
For him there weepeth bothe child and man.
So great a weeping was there none certain,
When Hector was y-brought, all fresh y-slain,
To Troy: alas! the pity that was there,
Scratching of cheeks, and rending eke of hair.
"Why wouldest thou be dead?" these women cry,
"And haddest gold enough, and Emily."
No manner man might gladden Theseus,
Saving his olde father Egeus,
That knew this worlde's transmutatioun,
As he had seen it changen up and down,
Joy after woe, and woe after gladness;
And shewed him example and likeness.
"Right as there died never man," quoth he,
"That he ne liv'd in earth in some degree*, *rank, condition
Right so there lived never man," he said,
"In all this world, that sometime be not died.
This world is but a throughfare full of woe,
And we be pilgrims, passing to and fro:
Death is an end of every worldly sore."
And over all this said he yet much more

To this effect, full wisely to exhort
The people, that they should them recomfort.
Duke Theseus, with all his busy cure*, *care
Casteth about, where that the sepulture *deliberates*
Of good Arcite may best y-maked be,
And eke most honourable in his degree.
And at the last he took conclusion,
That there as first Arcite and Palamon
Hadde for love the battle them between,
That in that selve* grove, sweet and green, *self-same
There as he had his amorous desires,
His complaint, and for love his hote fires,
He woulde make a fire*, in which th' office *funeral pyre
Of funeral he might all accomplice;
And *let anon command* to hack and hew *immediately
gave orders*
The oakes old, and lay them *on a rew* *in a row*
In culpons*, well arrayed for to brenne**. *logs **burn
His officers with swifte feet they renne* *run
And ride anon at his commandement.
And after this, Duke Theseus hath sent
After a bier, and it all oversprad
With cloth of gold, the richest that he had;
And of the same suit he clad Arcite.
Upon his handes were his gloves white,
Eke on his head a crown of laurel green,
And in his hand a sword full bright and keen.
He laid him *bare the visage* on the bier, *with face
uncovered*
Therewith he wept, that pity was to hear.
And, for the people shoulde see him all,
When it was day he brought them to the hall,
That roareth of the crying and the soun'.
Then came this woful Theban, Palamon,

With sluttery beard, and ruggy ashy hairs,<85>
In clothes black, y-dropped all with tears,
And (passing over weeping Emily)
The ruefullest of all the company.
And *inasmuch as* the service should be *in order that*
The more noble and rich in its degree,
Duke Theseus let forth three steedes bring,
That trapped were in steel all glittering.
And covered with the arms of Dan Arcite.
Upon these steedes, that were great and white,
There satte folk, of whom one bare his shield,
Another his spear in his handes held;
The thirde bare with him his bow Turkeis*, *Turkish.
Of brent* gold was the case** and the harness: *burnished
**quiver
And ride forth *a pace* with sorrowful cheer** *at a foot
pace*
Toward the grove, as ye shall after hear. **expression

The noblest of the Greekes that there were
Upon their shoulders carried the bier,
With slacke pace, and eyen red and wet,
Throughout the city, by the master* street, *main <86>
That spread was all with black, and wondrous high
Right of the same is all the street y-wrie.* *covered <87>
Upon the right hand went old Egeus,
And on the other side Duke Theseus,
With vessels in their hand of gold full fine,
All full of honey, milk, and blood, and wine;
Eke Palamon, with a great company;
And after that came woful Emily,
With fire in hand, as was that time the guise*, *custom
To do th' office of funeral service.

69

High labour, and full great appareling* *preparation
Was at the service, and the pyre-making,
That with its greene top the heaven raught*, *reached
And twenty fathom broad its armes straught*: *stretched
This is to say, the boughes were so broad.
Of straw first there was laid many a load.
But how the pyre was maked up on height,
And eke the names how the trees hight*, *were called
As oak, fir, birch, asp*, alder, holm, poplere, *aspen
Willow, elm, plane, ash, box, chestnut, lind*, laurere,
*linden, lime
Maple, thorn, beech, hazel, yew, whipul tree,
How they were fell'd, shall not be told for me;
Nor how the goddes* rannen up and down *the forest deities
Disinherited of their habitatioun,
In which they wonned* had in rest and peace, *dwelt
Nymphes, Faunes, and Hamadryades;
Nor how the beastes and the birdes all
Fledden for feare, when the wood gan fall;
Nor how the ground aghast* was of the light, *terrified
That was not wont to see the sunne bright;
Nor how the fire was couched* first with stre**, *laid
**straw
And then with dry stickes cloven in three,
And then with greene wood and spicery*, *spices
And then with cloth of gold and with pierrie*, *precious
stones
And garlands hanging with full many a flower,
The myrrh, the incense with so sweet odour;
Nor how Arcita lay among all this,
Nor what richess about his body is;
Nor how that Emily, as was the guise*, *custom
Put in the fire of funeral service<88>; *appplied the torch*
Nor how she swooned when she made the fire,

70

Nor what she spake, nor what was her desire;
Nor what jewels men in the fire then cast
When that the fire was great and burned fast;

Nor how some cast their shield, and some their spear,
And of their vestiments, which that they wear,
And cuppes full of wine, and milk, and blood,
Into the fire, that burnt as it were wood*; *mad
Nor how the Greekes with a huge rout* *procession
Three times riden all the fire about <89>
Upon the left hand, with a loud shouting,
And thries with their speares clattering;
And thries how the ladies gan to cry;
Nor how that led was homeward Emily;
Nor how Arcite is burnt to ashes cold;
Nor how the lyke-wake* was y-hold *wake <90>
All thilke* night, nor how the Greekes play *that
The wake-plays*, ne keep** I not to say: *funeral games
**care
Who wrestled best naked, with oil anoint,
Nor who that bare him best *in no disjoint*. *in any contest*
I will not tell eke how they all are gone
Home to Athenes when the play is done;
But shortly to the point now will I wend*, *come
And maken of my longe tale an end.

By process and by length of certain years
All stinted* is the mourning and the tears *ended
Of Greekes, by one general assent.
Then seemed me there was a parlement
At Athens, upon certain points and cas*: *cases
Amonge the which points y-spoken was
To have with certain countries alliance,
And have of Thebans full obeisance.

For which this noble Theseus anon
Let* send after the gentle Palamon, *caused
Unwist* of him what was the cause and why: *unknown
But in his blacke clothes sorrowfully
He came at his commandment *on hie*; *in haste*
Then sente Theseus for Emily.
When they were set*, and hush'd was all the place *seated
And Theseus abided* had a space *waited
Ere any word came from his wise breast
His eyen set he there as was his lest, *he cast his eyes
And with a sad visage he sighed still, wherever he pleased*
And after that right thus he said his will.
"The firste mover of the cause above
When he first made the faire chain of love,
Great was th' effect, and high was his intent;
Well wist he why, and what thereof he meant:
For with that faire chain of love he bond* *bound
The fire, the air, the water, and the lond
In certain bondes, that they may not flee:<91>
That same prince and mover eke," quoth he,
"Hath stablish'd, in this wretched world adown,
Certain of dayes and duration
To all that are engender'd in this place,
Over the whiche day they may not pace*, *pass
All may they yet their dayes well abridge.
There needeth no authority to allege
For it is proved by experience;
But that me list declare my sentence*. *opinion
Then may men by this order well discern,
That thilke* mover stable is and etern. *the same
Well may men know, but that it be a fool,
That every part deriveth from its whole.
For nature hath not ta'en its beginning
Of no *partie nor cantle* of a thing, *part or piece*

72

But of a thing that perfect is and stable,
Descending so, till it be corruptable.
And therefore of His wise purveyance* *providence
He hath so well beset* his ordinance,
That species of things and progressions
Shallen endure by successions,
And not etern, withouten any lie:
This mayst thou understand and see at eye.
Lo th' oak, that hath so long a nourishing
From the time that it 'ginneth first to spring,
And hath so long a life, as ye may see,
Yet at the last y-wasted is the tree.
Consider eke, how that the harde stone
Under our feet, on which we tread and gon*, *walk
Yet wasteth, as it lieth by the way.
The broade river some time waxeth drey*. *dry
The greate townes see we wane and wend*. *go, disappear
Then may ye see that all things have an end.
Of man and woman see we well also, —
That needes in one of the termes two, —
That is to say, in youth or else in age,-
He must be dead, the king as shall a page;
Some in his bed, some in the deepe sea,
Some in the large field, as ye may see:
There helpeth nought, all go that ilke* way: *same
Then may I say that alle thing must die.
What maketh this but Jupiter the king?
The which is prince, and cause of alle thing,
Converting all unto his proper will,
From which it is derived, sooth to tell
And hereagainst no creature alive,
Of no degree, availeth for to strive.
Then is it wisdom, as it thinketh me,
To make a virtue of necessity,

And take it well, that we may not eschew*, *escape
And namely what to us all is due.
And whoso grudgeth* ought, he doth folly, *murmurs at
And rebel is to him that all may gie*. *direct, guide
And certainly a man hath most honour
To dien in his excellence and flower,
When he is sicker* of his goode name. *certain
Then hath he done his friend, nor him*, no shame *himself
And gladder ought his friend be of his death,
When with honour is yielded up his breath,
Than when his name *appalled is for age*; *decayed by old
age*
For all forgotten is his vassalage*. *valour, service
Then is it best, as for a worthy fame,
To dien when a man is best of name.
The contrary of all this is wilfulness.
Why grudge we, why have we heaviness,
That good Arcite, of chivalry the flower,
Departed is, with duty and honour,
Out of this foule prison of this life?
Why grudge here his cousin and his wife
Of his welfare, that loved him so well?
Can he them thank? nay, God wot, neverdeal*, — *not a jot
That both his soul and eke themselves offend*, *hurt
And yet they may their lustes* not amend**. *desires
**control
What may I conclude of this longe serie*, *string of remarks
But after sorrow I rede* us to be merry, *counsel
And thanke Jupiter for all his grace?
And ere that we departe from this place,
I rede that we make of sorrows two
One perfect joye lasting evermo':
And look now where most sorrow is herein,
There will I first amenden and begin.

"Sister," quoth he, "this is my full assent,
With all th' advice here of my parlement,
That gentle Palamon, your owen knight,
That serveth you with will, and heart, and might,
And ever hath, since first time ye him knew,
That ye shall of your grace upon him rue*, *take pity
And take him for your husband and your lord:
Lend me your hand, for this is our accord.
Let see now of your womanly pity. *make display*
He is a kinge's brother's son, pardie*. *by God
And though he were a poore bachelere,
Since he hath served you so many a year,
And had for you so great adversity,
It muste be considered, *'lieveth me*. *believe me*
For gentle mercy *oweth to passen right*." *ought to be
rightly
Then said he thus to Palamon the knight; directed*
"I trow there needeth little sermoning
To make you assente to this thing.
Come near, and take your lady by the hand."
Betwixte them was made anon the band,
That hight matrimony or marriage,
By all the counsel of the baronage.
And thus with alle bliss and melody
Hath Palamon y-wedded Emily.
And God, that all this wide world hath wrought,
Send him his love, that hath it dearly bought.
For now is Palamon in all his weal,
Living in bliss, in riches, and in heal*. *health
And Emily him loves so tenderly,
And he her serveth all so gentilly,
That never was there worde them between
Of jealousy, nor of none other teen*. *cause of anger

Thus endeth Palamon and Emily
And God save all this faire company.

Notes to The Knight's Tale.

1. For the plan and principal incidents of the "Knight's Tale,"
Chaucer was indebted to Boccaccio, who had himself
borrowed from some prior poet, chronicler, or romancer.
Boccaccio speaks of the story as "very ancient;" and, though
that may not be proof of its antiquity, it certainly shows that
he took it from an earlier writer. The "Tale" is more or less a
paraphrase of Boccaccio's "Theseida;" but in some points the
copy has a distinct dramatic superiority over the original.
The "Theseida" contained ten thousand lines; Chaucer has
condensed it into less than one-fourth of the number. The
"Knight's Tale" is supposed to have been at first composed as
a separate work; it is undetermined whether Chaucer took it
direct from the Italian of Boccaccio, or from a French
translation.

2. Highte: was called; from the Anglo-Saxon "hatan", to bid
or call; German, "Heissen", "heisst".

3. Feminie: The "Royaume des Femmes" — kingdom of the
Amazons. Gower, in the "Confessio Amantis," styles
Penthesilea the "Queen of Feminie."

4. Wonnen: Won, conquered; German "gewonnen."

5. Ear: To plough; Latin, "arare." "I have abundant matter for
discourse." The first, and half of the second, of Boccaccio's
twelve books are disposed of in the few lines foregoing.

6. Waimenting: bewailing; German, "wehklagen"

7. Starf: died; German, "sterben," "starb".

8. The Minotaur: The monster, half-man and half-bull, which yearly devoured a tribute of fourteen Athenian youths and maidens, until it was slain by Theseus.

9. Pillers: pillagers, strippers; French, "pilleurs."

10. The donjon was originally the central tower or "keep" of feudal castles; it was employed to detain prisoners of importance. Hence the modern meaning of the word dungeon.

11. Saturn, in the old astrology, was a most unpropitious star to be born under.

12. To die in the pain was a proverbial expression in the French, used as an alternative to enforce a resolution or a promise. Edward III., according to Froissart, declared that he would either succeed in the war against France or die in the pain — "Ou il mourroit en la peine." It was the fashion in those times to swear oaths of friendship and brotherhood; and hence, though the fashion has long died out, we still speak of "sworn friends."

13. The saying of the old scholar Boethius, in his treatise "De Consolatione Philosophiae", which Chaucer translated, and from which he has freely borrowed in his poetry. The words are "Quis legem det amantibus? Major lex amor est sibi." ("Who can give law to lovers? Love is a law unto himself, and greater")

14. "Perithous" and "Theseus" must, for the metre, be pronounced as words of four and three syllables respectively — the vowels at the end not being diphthongated, but

enunciated separately, as if the words were printed Pe-ri-tho-us, The-se-us. The same rule applies in such words as "creature" and "conscience," which are trisyllables.

15. Stound: moment, short space of time; from Anglo-Saxon, "stund;" akin to which is German, "Stunde," an hour.

16. Meinie: servants, or menials, &c., dwelling together in a house; from an Anglo-Saxon word meaning a crowd. Compare German, "Menge," multitude.

17. The pure fetters: the very fetters. The Greeks used "katharos", the Romans "purus," in the same sense.

18. In the medieval courts of Love, to which allusion is probably made forty lines before, in the word "parlement," or "parliament," questions like that here proposed were seriously discussed.

19. Gear: behaviour, fashion, dress; but, by another reading, the word is "gyre," and means fit, trance — from the Latin, "gyro," I turn round.

20. Before his head in his cell fantastic: in front of his head in his cell of fantasy. "The division of the brain into cells, according to the different sensitive faculties," says Mr Wright, "is very ancient, and is found depicted in mediaeval manuscripts." In a manuscript in the Harleian Library, it is stated, "Certum est in prora cerebri esse fantasiam, in medio rationem discretionis, in puppi memoriam" (it is certain that in the front of the brain is imagination, in the middle reason, in the back memory) — a classification not materially differing from that of modern phrenologists.

21. Dan: Lord; Latin, "Dominus;" Spanish, "Don."

22. The "caduceus."

23. Argus was employed by Juno to watch Io with his hundred eyes but he was sent to sleep by the flute of Mercury, who then cut off his head.

24. Next: nearest; German, "naechste".

25. Clary: hippocras, wine made with spices.

26. Warray: make war; French "guerroyer", to molest; hence, perhaps, "to worry."

27. All day meeten men at unset steven: every day men meet at unexpected time. "To set a steven," is to fix a time, make an appointment.

28. Roundelay: song coming round again to the words with which it opened.

29. Now in the crop and now down in the breres: Now in the tree-top, now down in the briars. "Crop and root," top and bottom, is used to express the perfection or totality of anything.

30. Beknow: avow, acknowledge: German, "bekennen."

31. Shapen was my death erst than my shert: My death was decreed before my shirt ws shaped — that is, before any clothes were made for me, before my birth.

32. Regne: Queen; French, "Reine;" Venus is meant. The common reading, however, is "regne," reign or power.

33. Launde: plain. Compare modern English, "lawn," and French, "Landes" — flat, bare marshy tracts in the south of France.

34. Mister: manner, kind; German "muster," sample, model.

35. In listes: in the lists, prepared for such single combats between champion and accuser, &c.

36. Thilke: that, contracted from "the ilke," the same.

37. Mars the Red: referring to the ruddy colour of the planet, to which was doubtless due the transference to it of the name of the God of War. In his "Republic," enumerating the seven planets, Cicero speaks of the propitious and beneficent light of Jupiter: "Tum (fulgor) rutilis horribilisque terris, quem Martium dicitis" — "Then the red glow, horrible to the nations, which you say to be that of Mars." Boccaccio opens the "Theseida" by an invocation to "rubicondo Marte."

38. Last: lace, leash, noose, snare: from Latin, "laceus."

39. "Round was the shape, in manner of compass, Full of degrees, the height of sixty pas" The building was a circle of steps or benches, as in the ancient amphitheatre. Either the building was sixty paces high; or, more probably, there were sixty of the steps or benches.

40. Yellow goldes: The sunflower, turnsol, or girasol, which turns with and seems to watch the sun, as a jealous lover his mistress.

41. Citheron: The Isle of Venus, Cythera, in the Aegean Sea; now called Cerigo: not, as Chaucer's form of the word might imply, Mount Cithaeron, in the south-west of Boetia, which

was appropriated to other deities than Venus — to Jupiter, to Bacchus, and the Muses.

42. It need not be said that Chaucer pays slight heed to chronology in this passage, where the deeds of Turnus, the glory of King Solomon, and the fate of Croesus are made memories of the far past in the time of fabulous Theseus, the Minotaur-slayer.

43. Champartie: divided power or possession; an old law-term, signifying the maintenance of a person in a law suit on the condition of receiving part of the property in dispute, if recovered.

44. Citole: a kind of dulcimer.

45. The picke-purse: The plunderers that followed armies, and gave to war a horror all their own.

46. Shepen: stable; Anglo-Saxon, "scypen;" the word "sheppon" still survives in provincial parlance.

47. This line, perhaps, refers to the deed of Jael.

48. The shippes hoppesteres: The meaning is dubious. We may understand "the dancing ships," "the ships that hop" on the waves; "steres" being taken as the feminine adjectival termination: or we may, perhaps, read, with one of the manuscripts, "the ships upon the steres" — that is, even as they are being steered, or on the open sea — a more picturesque notion.

49. Freting: devouring; the Germans use "Fressen" to mean eating by animals, "essen" by men.

50. Julius: i.e. Julius Caesar

51. Puella and Rubeus were two figures in geomancy, representing two constellations-the one signifying Mars retrograde, the other Mars direct.

52. Calistope: or Callisto, daughter of Lycaon, seduced by Jupiter, turned into a bear by Diana, and placed afterwards, with her son, as the Great Bear among the stars.

53. Dane: Daphne, daughter of the river-god Peneus, in Thessaly; she was beloved by Apollo, but to avoid his pursuit, she was, at her own prayer, changed into a laurel-tree.

54. As the goddess of Light, or the goddess who brings to light, Diana — as well as Juno — was invoked by women in childbirth: so Horace, Odes iii. 22, says:—

"Montium custos nemorumque, Virgo,
Quae laborantes utero puellas
Ter vocata audis adimisque leto,
Diva triformis."

("Virgin custodian of hills and groves, three-formed goddess who hears and saves from death young women who call upon her thrice when in childbirth")

55. Every deal: in every part; "deal" corresponds to the German "Theil" a portion.

56. Sikerly: surely; German, "sicher;" Scotch, "sikkar," certain. When Robert Bruce had escaped from England to assume the Scottish crown, he stabbed Comyn before the altar at Dumfries; and, emerging from the church, was asked

by his friend Kirkpatrick if he had slain the traitor. "I doubt it," said Bruce. "Doubt," cried Kirkpatrick. "I'll mak sikkar;" and he rushed into the church, and despatched Comyn with repeated thrusts of his dagger.

57. Kemped: combed; the word survives in "unkempt."

58. Alauns: greyhounds, mastiffs; from the Spanish word "Alano," signifying a mastiff.

59. Y-ment: mixed; German, "mengen," to mix.

60. Prime: The time of early prayers, between six and nine in the morning.

61. On the dais: see note 32 to the Prologue.

62. In her hour: in the hour of the day (two hours before daybreak) which after the astrological system that divided the twenty-four among the seven ruling planets, was under the influence of Venus.

63. Adon: Adonis, a beautiful youth beloved of Venus, whose death by the tusk of a boar she deeply mourned.

64. The third hour unequal: In the third planetary hour; Palamon had gone forth in the hour of Venus, two hours before daybreak; the hour of Mercury intervened; the third hour was that of Luna, or Diana. "Unequal" refers to the astrological division of day and night, whatever their duration, into twelve parts, which of necessity varied in length with the season.

65. Smoking: draping; hence the word "smock;" "smokless," in Chaucer, means naked.

66. Cerrial: of the species of oak which Pliny, in his "Natural History," calls "cerrus."

67. Stace of Thebes: Statius, the Roman who embodied in the twelve books of his "Thebaid" the ancient legends connected with the war of the seven against Thebes.

68. Diana was Luna in heaven, Diana on earth, and Hecate in hell; hence the direction of the eyes of her statue to "Pluto's dark region." Her statue was set up where three ways met, so that with a different face she looked down each of the three; from which she was called Trivia. See the quotation from Horace, note 54.

69. Las: net; the invisible toils in which Hephaestus caught Ares and the faithless Aphrodite, and exposed them to the "inextinguishable laughter" of Olympus.

70. Saturnus the cold: Here, as in "Mars the Red" we have the person of the deity endowed with the supposed quality of the planet called after his name.

71. The astrologers ascribed great power to Saturn, and predicted "much debate" under his ascendancy; hence it was "against his kind" to compose the heavenly strife.

72. Ayel: grandfather; French "Aieul".

73. Testers: Helmets; from the French "teste", "tete", head.

74. Parements: ornamental garb, French "parer" to deck.

75. Gniding: Rubbing, polishing; Anglo-Saxon "gnidan", to rub.

76. Nakeres: Drums, used in the cavalry; Boccaccio's word is "nachere".

77. Made an O: Ho! Ho! to command attention; like "oyez", the call for silence in law-courts or before proclamations.

78. Sarge: serge, a coarse woollen cloth

79. Heart-spoon: The concave part of the breast, where the lower ribs join the cartilago ensiformis.

80. To-hewen and to-shred: "to" before a verb implies extraordinary violence in the action denoted.

81. He through the thickest of the throng etc.. "He" in this passage refers impersonally to any of the combatants.

82. Galaphay: Galapha, in Mauritania.

83. Belmarie is supposed to have been a Moorish state in Africa; but "Palmyrie" has been suggested as the correct reading.

84. As I came never I cannot telle where: Where it went I cannot tell you, as I was not there. Tyrwhitt thinks that Chaucer is sneering at Boccacio's pompous account of the passage of Arcite's soul to heaven. Up to this point, the description of the death-scene is taken literally from the "Theseida."

85. With sluttery beard, and ruggy ashy hairs: With neglected beard, and rough hair strewn with ashes. "Flotery" is the general reading; but "sluttery" seems to be more in keeping with the picture of abandonment to grief.

86. Master street: main street; so Froissart speaks of "le souverain carrefour."

87. Y-wrie: covered, hid; Anglo-Saxon, "wrigan," to veil.

88. Emily applied the funeral torch. The "guise" was, among the ancients, for the nearest relative of the deceased to do this, with averted face.

89. It was the custom for soldiers to march thrice around the funeral pile of an emperor or general; "on the left hand" is added, in reference to the belief that the left hand was propitious — the Roman augur turning his face southward, and so placing on his left hand the east, whence good omens came. With the Greeks, however, their augurs facing the north, it was just the contrary. The confusion, frequent in classical writers, is complicated here by the fact that Chaucer's description of the funeral of Arcite is taken from Statius' "Thebaid" — from a Roman's account of a Greek solemnity.

90. Lyke-wake: watching by the remains of the dead; from Anglo-Saxon, "lice," a corpse; German, "Leichnam."

91. Chaucer here borrows from Boethius, who says: "Hanc rerum seriem ligat, Terras ac pelagus regens, Et coelo imperitans, amor." (Love ties these things together: the earth, and the ruling sea, and the imperial heavens)

MLA Style Citations for Scholarly Secondary Sources, Peer-Reviewed Journal Articles and Critical Essays for The Knight's Tale

Ackerman, Robert W. "Tester: Knight's Tale, 2499." *Modern Language Notes*, vol. 49, no. 6, 1934, pp. 397–400. www.jstor.org/stable/2912885.

Al-Saleh, Asaad. "Fate and Discipline: A Comparative Study of 'The Tale of the Heike' and Chaucer's 'The Knight's Tale'." *The Journal of the Midwest Modern Language Association*, vol. 45, no. 1, 2012, pp. 35–57. www.jstor.org/stable/43150829.

Frost, William. "An Interpretation of Chaucer's Knight's Tale." *The Review of English Studies*, vol. 25, no. 100, 1949, pp. 289–304. www.jstor.org/stable/511478.

Gibbs, Lincoln R. "The Meaning of Feeldes in Chaucer's Knight's Tale, Vv. 975-977." *Modern Language Notes*, vol. 24, no. 7, 1909, pp. 197–198. www.jstor.org/stable/2916554.

Ham, Edward B. "Knight's Tale 38." *ELH*, vol. 17, no. 4, 1950, pp. 252–261. www.jstor.org/stable/2872049.

Helterman, Jeffrey. "The Dehumanizing Metamorphoses of The Knight's Tale." *ELH*, vol. 38, no. 4, 1971, pp. 493–511. www.jstor.org/stable/2872262.

Langmuir, Gavin I. "The Knight's Tale of Young Hugh of Lincoln." *Speculum*, vol. 47, no. 3, 1972, pp. 459–482. www.jstor.org/stable/2856155.

Madden, William A. "'Some Philosophical Aspects of the Knight's Tale': A Reply." *College English*, vol. 20, no. 4, 1959, pp. 193–194. www.jstor.org/stable/372266.

Mitchell, Edward R. "The Two Mayings in Chaucer's 'Knight's Tale.'" *Modern Language Notes*, vol. 71, no. 8, 1956, pp. 560–564. www.jstor.org/stable/3043624.

Muscatine, Charles. "Form, Texture, and Meaning in Chaucer's Knight's Tale." *PMLA*, vol. 65, no. 5, 1950, pp. 911–929. www.jstor.org/stable/459581.

Parr, Johnstone. "The Date and Revision of Chaucer's Knight's Tale." *PMLA*, vol. 60, no. 2, 1945, pp. 307–324. www.jstor.org/stable/459073.

Pratt, Robert A., and Johnstone Parr. "Was Chaucer's Knight's Tale Extensively Revised after the Middle of 1390?" *PMLA*, vol. 63, no. 2, 1948, pp. 726–739. www.jstor.org/stable/459440.

Robertson, Stuart. "Elements of Realism in the 'Knight's Tale.'." *The Journal of English and Germanic Philology*, vol. 14, no. 2, 1915, pp. 226–255. www.jstor.org/stable/27700659.

Ruggiers, Paul G. "Some Philosophical Aspects of the Knight's Tale." *College English*, vol. 19, no. 7, 1958, pp. 296–302. www.jstor.org/stable/371632.

Smith, Roland M. "Three Notes on the Knight's Tale." *Modern Language Notes*, vol. 51, no. 5, 1936, pp. 318–322. www.jstor.org/stable/2912648.

Von Kreisler, Nicolai. "A Recurrent Expression of Devotion in Chaucer's 'Book of the Duchess," 'Parliament of Fowls," and 'Knight's Tale.'" *Modern Philology*, vol. 68, no. 1, 1970, pp. 62–64. www.jstor.org/stable/436303.

Wager, Willis J. "The So-Called Prologue to the Knight's Tale." *Modern Language Notes*, vol. 50, no. 5, 1935, pp. 296–307. www.jstor.org/stable/2912511.

MLA Style Citations for Scholarly Secondary Sources, Peer-Reviewed Journal Articles and Critical Essays for The Canterbury Tales Overall

Biggs, Frederick M. "The Miller's Tale and Decameron 3.4." *The Journal of English and Germanic Philology* 108.1 (2009): 59+. *Literature Resource Center*. Web.

Blamires, Alcuin. "The Wife of Bath and Lollardy." *Medium Aevum* 58.2 (1989): 224-242. Rpt. in *Poetry Criticism*. Ed. Lawrence J. Trudeau. Vol. 58. Detroit: Gale, 2005. *Poetry Criticism Online*. Web.

Blamires, Alcuin. "Philosophical sleaze? The 'strok of thought' in the Miller's Tale and Chaucerian fabliau." *The Modern Language Review* 102.3 (2007): 621+. *Literature Resource Center*. Web.

Chance, Jane. "Representing rebellion: the ending of Chaucer's Knight's Tale and the castration of Saturn (1)." *Studia Anglica Posnaniensia: International Review of English Studies* 38 (2002): 75+. *Literature Resource Center*. Web.

Cooper, Helen. *The Canterbury Tales* (Oxford: Oxford University Press, 1996).

Cooper, Helen. *The Structure of the Canterbury Tales* (Athens, Ga.: University of Georgia Press, 1984).

Cox, Catherine S. "Holy Erotica and the Virgin Word: Promiscuous Glossing in the Wife of Bath's Prologue." *Exemplaria* 5.1 (Mar. 1993): 207-237. Rpt. in *Poetry Criticism*. Ed. Lawrence J. Trudeau. Vol. 58. Detroit: Gale, 2005. *Poetry Criticism Online*. Web.

Czarnowus, Anna. "Chaucer's clergeon, or towards holiness in The Prioress's Tale." *Studia Anglica Posnaniensia: International Review of English Studies* 43 (2007): 251+. *Literature Resource Center*. Web.

D'Arcy, Anne Marie. "'Cursed folk of herodes al new': supersessionist typology and Chaucer's prioress." *Essays and Studies* (2002): 117+. *Literature Resource Center*. Web.

Dobbs, Elizabeth A. "The Canaanite woman, the Second Nun, and St. Cecilia." *Christianity and Literature* 62.2 (2013): 203+. *Literature Resource Center*. Web.

Eaton, R.D. "Sin and sensibility: the conscience of Chaucer's Prioress." *The Journal of English and Germanic Philology* 104.4 (2005): 495+. *Literature Resource Center*. Web.

Fleming, John V. "Chaucer and Erasmus on the Pilgrimage to Canterbury: An Iconographical Speculation." *The Popular Literature of Medieval England*. Ed. Thomas J. Heffernan. Knoxville: University of Tennessee Press, 1985. 148-166. Rpt. in *Classical and Medieval Literature Criticism*. Ed. Jelena O. Krstovic. Vol. 115. Detroit: Gale, 2010. *Literature Resource Center*. Web.

Gruenler, Curtis. "Desire, Violence and the Passion in Fragment VII of the Canterbury Tales: A Girardian Reading."*Renascence: Essays on Values in Literature* 52.1 (1999): 35. *Literature Resource Center*. Web.

Ireland, Colin A. "'A Coverchief or a Calle': The Ultimate End of the Wife of Bath's Search for Sovereignty." *Neophilologus* 75.1 (Jan. 1991): 150-159. Rpt. in *Poetry Criticism*. Ed. Lawrence J. Trudeau. Vol. 58. Detroit: Gale, 2005. *Literature Resource Center*. Web.

Ladd, Roger A. "The mercantile (mis)reader in The Canterbury Tales." *Studies in Philology* 99.1 (2002): 17+. *Literature Resource Center*. Web.

Lambdin, Laura C. and Robert T. Lambdin, eds., *Chaucer's Pilgrims: An Historical Guide to the Pilgrims in TheCanterbury Tales* (Westport, Conn.: Greenwood Press, 1996).

McGalliard, John C. "Chaucerian Comedy: *The Merchant's Tale,* Jonson, and Molière." *Philological Quarterly* 25.4 (Oct. 1946): 343-370. Rpt. in *Literature Criticism from 1400 to 1800.* Ed. Michael L. LaBlanc. Vol. 85. Detroit: Gale, 2003. *Literature Resource Center.* Web.

Morgan, Gerald. "The logic of the Clerk's Tale." *The Modern Language Review* 104.1 (2009): 1+. *Literature Resource Center.* Web.

Morrison, Susan Signe. "Don't Ask, Don't Tell: The Wife of Bath and Vernacular Translations." *Exemplaria* 8.1 (Spring 1996): 97-123. Rpt. in *Poetry Criticism.* Ed. Lawrence J. Trudeau. Vol. 58. Detroit: Gale, 2005. *Literature Resource Center.* Web.

Norsworthy, Scott. "Hard lords and bad food-service in the Monk's Tale." *The Journal of English and Germanic Philology* 100.3 (2001): 313+. *Literature Resource Center.* Web.

O'Brien, Timothy D. "Seductive Violence and Three Chaucerian Women." *College Literature* 28.2 (2001): 178. *Literature Resource Center.* Web.

Pearcy, Roy J. "Anglo-Norman Fabliaux and Chaucer's Merchant's Tale." *Medium Aevum* 69.2 (2000): 227. *Literature Resource Center*. Web.

Pearsall, Derek. *The Canterbury Tales* (London: Allen and Unwin, 1985).

Rigby, S. H. "Misogynist versus Feminist Chaucer." *Chaucer in Context: Society, Allegory and Gender.* Manchester University Press, 1996. 116-163. Rpt. in *Literature Criticism from 1400 to 1800*. Ed. Lawrence J. Trudeau. Vol. 56. Detroit: Gale, 2000. *Literature Resource Center*. Web.

Robinson, Ian. "Chaucer's Religious Tales." *The Critical Review* 10 (1967): 18-32. Rpt. in *Poetry Criticism*. Ed. Carol T. Gaffke. Vol. 19. Detroit: Gale, 1997. *Literature Resource Center*. Web.

Ruggiers, Paul G. *The Art of the Canterbury Tales* (Madison, Wisc.: University of Wisconsin Press, 1965).

Tasioulas, Jacqueline. "'Dying of imagination' in the First Fragment of the Canterbury Tales." *Medium Aevum* 82.2 (2013): 213+. *Literature Resource Center*. Web.

"The Canterbury Tales." *Arts and Humanities Through the Eras*. Ed. Edward I. Bleiberg, et al. Vol. 3: Medieval Europe 814-1450. Detroit: Gale, 2005. 199-201. *Gale Virtual Reference Library*. Web.

"*The Wife of Bath's Prologue* and *Tale*." *Poetry Criticism*. Ed. Lawrence J. Trudeau. Vol. 58. Detroit: Gale, 2005. *Literature Resource Center*. Web.

Thompson, N. S. "Local Histories: Characteristic Worlds in the *Decameron* and the *Canterbury Tales*." *The Decameron and the Canterbury Tales: New Essays on an Old Question*. Ed. Leonard Michael Koff and Brenda Deen Schildgen. Madison, N.J.: Fairleigh Dickinson University Press, 2000. 85-101. Rpt. in *Short Story Criticism*. Ed. Thomas J. Schoenberg and Lawrence J. Trudeau. Vol. 87. Detroit: Gale, 2006. *Literature Resource Center*. Web.

Treharne, Elaine. "The Stereotype Confirmed? Chaucer's Wife of Bath." *Writing Gender and Genre in Medieval Literature: Approaches to Old and Middle English Texts*. Ed. Elaine Treharne. Cambridge: D. S. Brewer, 2002. 93-115. Rpt. in *Poetry Criticism*. Ed. Lawrence J. Trudeau. Vol. 58. Detroit: Gale, 2005. *Literature Resource Center*. Web.

Wadiak, Walter. "Chaucer's Knight's Tale and the politics of distinction." *Philological Quarterly* 89.2-3 (2010): 159+. *Literature Resource Center*. Web.

WAUGH, ROBIN. "A Woman in the Mind's Eye (and not): Narrators and Gazes in Chaucer's Clerk's Tale and in Two Analogues." *Philological Quarterly* 79.1 (2000): 1. *Literature Resource Center*. Web.

Wilsbacher, Greg. "Lumiansky's paradox: ethics, aesthetics and Chaucer's 'Prioress's Tale'." *College Literature* 32.4 (2005): 1+. *Literature Resource Center*. Web.

Printed in Great Britain
by Amazon